GW01511118

AN INDIAN TABLE

AN INDIAN TABLE

A FAMILY'S RECIPES DURING THE RAJ

BRYONY HILL

Red Door

Published by RedDoor
www.reddoorpress.co.uk
© 2021 Bryony Hill

The right of Bryony Hill to be identified as author of this Work has been asserted by her in accordance with sections 77 and 78 of the Copyright, Designs and Patents Act 1988

Every effort has been made to trace copyright holders and to obtain their permission for the use of copyright material. The author and publisher apologise for any errors or omissions and would be grateful if notified of any corrections that should be incorporated in future reprints or editions of this book

978-1-913062-60-6

All rights reserved. No part of this publication may be reproduced, stored in a retrieval system, copied in any form or by any means, electronic, mechanical, photocopying, recording or otherwise transmitted without written permission from the author

A CIP catalogue record for this book is available from the British Library

Cover design: Emily Courdelle
Typesetting: Megan Sheer

Printed and bound in Poland by BZGraf S.A.

Contents

Foreword 7

Prologue 11

Indian Weights and Measures 15

Basic Cooking Tips 17

Table of Proportions 21

Spices and Condiments 25

Sauces and Stuffings 41

Soups 61

Fish 71

Meat and Poultry 83

Vegetable and Savoury Dishes 109

Puddings 137

Cakes 165

Biscuits, Breads and Buns 191

Preserves, Jams and Chutneys 205

Beverages and Cocktails 219

Index 225

About the Author 238

Acknowledgements 239

Foreword

It is intriguing that even though these family recipes may no longer be relevant to modern day cooking, the way they have been reasoned with and created leaves one full of inspiration and awe. I can well imagine the domestics, maids and other help scurrying about lighting the fires, keeping the logs burning and working in a smoky, hot, sticky environment.

While I am a child of the fifties, I did spend a few years of my life in my uncle's home in Rajasthan. I remember the old kitchen with fires lit, on which logs and dung cakes were burnt, with pails of water on them for bathing purposes. On those same fires, fresh hot chapatis were made daily and a special kind of bread, an unleavened dough often known as *baati*, was buried below the ash to cook slowly until crisp and baked.

In my ancestral home we had one of these old range-type cookers, fired with wood, plus a discarded one which had multiple ovens and plates on top. I have no idea how they made it across the sea to India, nor how they were installed, but I liked to play with the redundant one. Some of the ovens were so large a child could hide inside – so that's what we did.

The recipes in Bryony's book sound delicious and with such liberal use of curry powder (that was originally created for a certain Colonel Bolst in Madras), I can understand how the love for this ingredient travelled to Britain. As the lore goes, curry powder was created for Colonel Bolst when he returned to England from his posting. Eager to impress his friends, the colonel asked his local spice merchant to recreate the powder for his cooks. One must note that back in those days food such as bananas, cashew nuts and sultanas, for example, were considered a luxury that only the wealthy could afford. This is how such ingredients that did not feature in the original Indian dish made their way into the classic English curry, much softened by the fruits and with flour added to thicken the sauce. Thus followed a surge in popularity of the English curry in the military households. The spice merchant named the powder after the Colonel – and the name stuck.

Bryony's recipes are full of the traditions of the past and capture the very essence of Calcutta as it was then and still is today. For example, fears of undercooked seafood and bacterial infection of raw meat due to lack of refrigeration in the sultry heat and humidity. Bryony's ancestors must have been exposed to that diehard fish-eating, mustard-oil-reeking and mustard-zinging culture. It is little wonder then that from the Calcutta experience the humble mustard found its way into Britain to become so much a part of the British mainstream diet. While perhaps originally used to smother the rot in the food, it has since emerged as the super-exciting, awakening condiment that it really is.

There is more to learn from this recipe book – not just about what the British household ate when living and entertaining in India but also what the gradual acceptance of Indian herbs and spices did to their diets, which evolved into a completely different form of cooking. For example, parsley. I am sure that parsley was grown and consumed at that time in the land where coriander was and still is king. Cucumber in a prawn curry? Who ever thought of that? That's now a must try – I want to see what it does to a prawn curry. Would I have ever tried that before now? Absolutely not! But seeing how it was done and why, I am now a convert. Another revelation is the liberal use of ghee in all the cooking and the lesser use of the local mustard oil or other cold-pressed oils. I would never have used ghee with prawns, nor would I cook them for so long but I suppose when compared to mustard oil, ghee is definitely the preferred choice for prawns.

I could go on but I will let the reader make their own judgement and experience their own journey into a world that may no longer exist, but which can be reawakened by trying the many recipes here and adapting them to suit modern tastes, availability and new cooking methods.

The water colour images depict life as it was then and the recipes collectively give an impression, a vision and an insight into life and cooking in the nineteenth and twentieth centuries in the British household in India. For a chef who is forever seeking new knowledge and insights this book is inspirational and these works would have been lost to the world had that attic and its contents not been put to print and shared with the world.

I wish the new book much success so that more people, especially from the younger generations, can see the links and relationships that ran so deeply in our two cultures.

Cyrus Rustom Todiwala OBE DL DBA

Prologue

... And there was the alien food of India. Those who rejected its flavours discovered their choices were limited because so many ingredients, which constituted the familiar fare on British menus, were not available. Here we have a unique record of one British family who left the Highlands for India whose recipes are naturally fascinating, showing how those preparing meals coped with the limitations India imposed on their choice.

Sir Mark Tully KBE, former Bureau Chief of BBC, New Delhi

Some of you will be familiar with my memoir *Scotland to Shalimar – A Family's Life in India* (RedDoor Press, 2020), which was inspired first by two albums full of exquisite watercolours and sketches and second by the discovery of my 3 x great-grandmother Frances Charlotte Campbell's, great-great-grandmother Emily Frances Margaret Begbie's (née Campbell) and my great-grandmother Eleanor 'Nell' Geraldine Birch's (née Begbie) collection of recipes. These treasures remained hidden for decades in the attic of our old family home until they came to light after my mother died in 2007. I included a small selection, the tip of an iceberg, in the first book but now I want to share all of them with a wider audience in the knowledge that they might bring back nostalgic memories to those who had lived in India during and after the Raj.

Many of the recipes were recorded by Emily in the late 1800s before she married my great-great-grandfather Col Francis Richard Begbie, both forebears contributing liberally to the albums with their enchanting watercolour paintings and sketches. The first album was started circa 1818 by my 4 x great-grandmother Margaret Anna Grant after she arrived in India from Scotland with her father James Grant of Dalvey. James was employed by the Honourable East India Company and, a few years afterwards, Margaret Anna married Alfred William Begbie in Allahabad in August 1824. Their daughter Frances 'Fanny' Charlotte Begbie, my 3 x great-grandmother (the first of six generations to be born in India), was given her own album on her wedding day in 1847 as a gift from her husband John Peter William Campbell; many of the floral illustrations are painted by her and also by the hand of John Peter William during the Umbeyla campaign in 1863.

Above left: *Frances Charlotte Campbell, my 3 x great-grandmother*

Above right: *John Peter William Campbell, my 3 x great-grandfather*

Emily Frances Begbie (née Campbell) as a young woman and in her mature years, my great-great-grandmother

Emily and Nell were both excellent, instinctive cooks, which explains why many of the recipes are bereft of detailed instructions not least because cooking facilities were basic in the extreme: the wood-fired oven was either piping hot or stone cold and the only way to adjust the temperature was to leave the oven door ajar.

Access to fresh produce and supplies was haphazard and preserving foodstuffs by pickling, salting and bottling was a vital necessity. Also, because of the unhospitable, sweltering climate, the hearty stews, wholesome curries and rich fruit cakes seem incongruous. All was explained when I learned that the family moved from the plains to the higher altitudes during the summer months to escape the stultifying heat. Snow could be on the ground and they needed heart and tummy-warming offerings, log fires and blankets to compensate for chillier nights. Some of these recipes might represent more of a curiosity to our twenty-first-century tastes but others remain family favourites to this day. I found myself faced with a conundrum: should I keep them in their original form as they were jotted down 150 years ago in India by Fanny, Emily and Nell or should I bring them up to date? In the end, after much deliberation, I decided to reproduce their culinary shorthand verbatim in order to retain authenticity and the sense of period. Judging by many of the dishes, mealtimes around the family table were never a dull affair.

Eleanor 'Nell' Geraldine Birch (née Begbie) my great-grandmother

Indian Weights and Measures

The unit here [in India] is a tablespoon but any measure either of capacity or weight may be substituted – each egg is counted as 2 units: white = 1 unit, yolk = 1 unit. The unit here in the receipts [recipes] is 1 tablespoon pressed down lightly for solids and as full as it can be for liquids. That is to say, approximately 1 oz, if that measure be prepared. This gives a result suitable for two or three people. For all things that can be measured in a tablespoon, the unit is a tablespoon. For such things, as cannot be measured in a tablespoon the unit is 1 oz – this is mostly stock and 5 units raw meat and 20 units water means 5 oz raw meat and 20 tablespoons water.

A chittack is an old Indian weight or measure the equivalent of 1 oz, while a gill is equivalent to ¼ pint and a seer is approximately 2¼ lb.

Basic Cooking Tips

BOILING

Meat should be put into water that is boiling furiously and kept boiling like this for 5 minutes. This makes outside of meat hard and preserves juice inside. After 5 minutes, simmer gently.

FISH

Never use very hot water or the skin will break. Vinegar and salt should always be in the water. To make very good boiling liquor for it: water, vinegar, claret, onions and carrots and a faggot of herbs boiled together and allowed to get cold. Then strain off and use to boil your fish in.

VEGETABLES

They should be not washed till they are to be cooked and they should be plunged into boiling water into which 1 dessertspoon of salt has been added to 1 quart of water. The saucepan should be uncovered and they should boil furiously.

PEAS AND BEANS

They require a teaspoonful of sugar in addition to the salt.

POTATOES

They should always be put in cold water and only just enough to cover them and after first boil cannot simmer too slowly. They require at least one hour to dry after the water has been drained off.

SOUFFLES

To prevent sinking: place on dish on which there is heated salt. Wonderful in its effects.

SOUPS

To remove fat: dip a clean dinner napkin in cold water, wring it out and drop on surface of broth. Remove.

COFFEE

Warm jug. Put in coffee. Pour in boiling water and beat with wooden spoon till the grounds sink.

CAKE OR LOAF WHEN STALE

To make fresh: throw a teacup of water into a hot oven. Place the cake or loaf in the oven, shut the door and in ten minutes it will be quite fresh. There is no fear of rusting oven.

CAKE, TO PREVENT STICKING TO A TIN

Place the tin on a damp cloth when you take it out of the oven and the cake will be in no danger of sticking.

CAKE, TO KEEP MOIST

Place in a tin with a thick slice of bread at the top and bottom of the tin. The bread will become hard as a rock. The cake having drained all the moisture away from the bread will be quite fresh. Or place butterproof paper all round the tin and put the cake in it.

To prevent illness, all uncooked food (salads, fruit, etc.) was given a brief soak in 'pinky pani', the name given to a dilute solution of potassium permanganate, which was lethal to micro-organisms.

Table of Proportions

BATTER	Baked or boiled: 4 units flour, 4 units eggs, 16 units milk.
FRYING BATTER	1 unit flour, 2 units liquid, 1 egg, ¼ oz oil.
SOUFFLE BATTER	For the roux: Boil 1 unit water with ¼ unit butter, then add 1 unit flour and beat. When cool, beat in 1 egg yolk then fold in whisked egg white. Fry.
CAKES	A standard cake: 16 units self-raising flour, 12 units sugar, 8 units butter, 5 eggs.
CUSTARDS	Baked: 3 eggs to 20 units milk. Bake 8–20 minutes.

FARINES	Cornflour: 1½ units to 20 units liquid. Rice: 8 units to 20 units. Sago: 4 units to 20 units. Ground rice: 6 units to 20 units. Tapioca: 3 units to 20 units.
GELATINE	Jellies: 1 unit ground gelatine to 20 units liquid; Creams: 2 units or 1 unit to 24 units.
MEAT MOULDS	Raw meat: 1 unit to 2 units milk or stock. Cooked meat: 2 units meat, 1 unit panade, 1 unit milk, ½ unit egg.
MILK PUDDINGS	Cornflour: 1 unit to 20 units liquid. Arrowroot: 1 unit to 20 units. Rice: 3 units to 20 units. Sago, semolina and tapioca: 2 units to 20 units. Macaroni and vermicelli: 4 (solid) units to 20 units.
PASTRY	Puff: 4 units butter to 4 units flour. Medium: 3 units butter to 4 units flour. Family: 2 units butter to 4 units flour. Short: 2 units butter to 4 units flour, 1 unit sugar. Suet: 5 units suet to 8 units flour.

STOCK	Ordinary: 16 units meat or fish (solid) to 44 units liquid. Add 8 units meat for best consommés.
THICKENING	Soups: ½ unit to 1 unit flour to 44 units liquid.
	Ordinary sauces: 1 unit flour, 1 unit butter to 15 units liquid.
	Thick: 1 unit flour, 1 unit butter to 12 units liquid.
	Thin: 1 unit flour, 1 unit butter to 20 units liquid.

Spices and Condiments

GHEE

Melt 1 lb of the best unsalted butter you can find – the better the butter, the better the ghee. This will give you approximately ¾ lb of ghee. Break up 1 lb butter and put into a saucepan with 2 bay leaves and a few cloves. Bring to the boil, the water will evaporate and the butter will separate, leaving sediment on the bottom of the pan. Continue boiling (but do not stir) until the clear butter stops making a noise and the sediment begins to take on a light brown colour. This may take a little more than 15 minutes. Remove from the heat and allow to cool a little but while still hot pass through a sieve lined with a fine muslin cloth. Pour into sterilised jars, cover and keep in a cool place. Once cold the ghee will turn hard and is an opaque yellow. It will last indefinitely.

MADRAS CURRY POWDER

Mix together 8 units each of: coriander (*dhaniya*), turmeric (*haldee*), cumin (*jeera*)

Add 4 units each of: pepper (*mirch*) and dry sugar (*sookhee cheeni*)

Add 2 units each of: fenugreek (*menthee*), cardamoms (*ilnayachee*), chillies (*lal mirch*), mace (*jowtri gada*)

Add 1 unit each of: poppy seeds (*khasa khas*), mustard seed (*sarason ke beej*), cloves (*kaung*)

Excellent.

SPICE SALT

* 2 units each of powdered nutmeg and cloves
* 1 unit each of powdered pepper and chillies

Mix 2 units of this with 8 units of table salt. A teaspoon in a dish is enough. Useful for the cook.

CURRY PASTE

* 8 oz roasted coriander seeds
* 1 oz cumin seeds
* 2 oz turmeric
* 2 oz dry chillies
* 2 oz black pepper
* 2 oz mustard seed
* 1 oz dry ginger
* 4 oz dried lentils

Pound all the ingredients together in a mortar with the best English white wine vinegar to the consistency of a thick jelly. Warm some good oil and when hot, fry until it is reduced to a thick paste. Allow to cool and put into sterilised bottles. Do not use any water in the preparation. Mustard oil is better adapted for frying the mixture. This makes a nice gift.

FRANCATELLI'S* HERB SEASONING

* 1 oz nutmeg
* 1 oz mace
* 2 oz cloves
* 2 oz peppercorns
* 1 oz dried bay leaves
* 3 oz basil
* 3 oz marjoram
* 2 oz winter savory
* 3 oz thyme
* ½ oz cayenne pepper
* ½ oz grated lemon peel
* 2 cloves of garlic

All to be well pounded in a mortar and passed through a wire sieve, put away to dry, well-corked later. This seasoning is very delicious and can be used whenever the fresh herbs are ordered in the receipt.

* Charles Elmé Francatelli (1805–76) was chief cook to Her Majesty Queen Victoria.

DEVIL MIXTURE

For any kind of grill, also for seasoning steaks, butter, sauce, etc.

* 1 spoonful made (Kancha English) mustard
* 1 spoonful King of Oudh sauce [King of Oudh sauce is no longer available commercially but chutney is a good substitute]
* 1 spoonful anchovy sauce [recipe page 42]
* 1 spoonful salad oil
* ½ spoonful cayenne

Mix all the ingredients well together. Deeply score the meat or fish you wish to grill. Cover with the sauce and grill or fry till brown.

FRESH COCONUT MILK

Get a coconut. Break it, scrape the centre into a small bowl. Pour boiling water over it and allow it to steep for 10–20 minutes, then strain through a piece of muslin into another basin. It is now ready to use. Throw away the coconut pulp.

MALAY SPICE POWDER

* 24 units turmeric
* 16 units dry ginger
* 4 units chillies
* 8 units cardamoms
* 1 unit cloves
* 1 unit cinnamon

Pound all the ingredients together. Malay curries are invariably made with coconut milk [see page 29]. Garlic must be used and the cloves and cinnamon increased if a spice flavour is desired.

CAYENNE SALT

1 unit of cayenne pepper boiled in 20 units of water and strained. Saturate the water with salt and evaporate in the sun. When it crystallises, grind to a powder and put away for use. It may be coloured red.

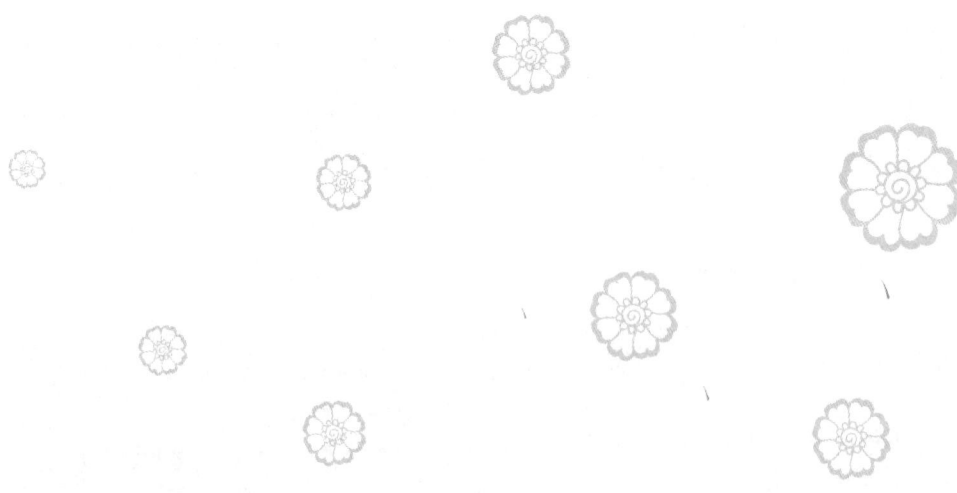

VINEGARS

Vinegars are very useful for cooking and may be made by steeping herbs: parsley, thyme, rosemary, tarragon or mint in vinegar for several days. The proportion is 3 units of leaves to 20 units of vinegar. The following is excellent in 30 units of vinegar. Steep for 14 days.

* 5 cloves
* 2 cloves of garlic
* 1 lime in slices (the thick-skinned kind)
* A small handful of thyme and savory and, if possible, tarragon and 1 green chilli

Decant and bottle.

SPICED VINEGAR FOR PICKLED ONIONS

* 1 pint vinegar
* ½ oz whole cloves
* ¼ oz mixed spices
* 3-4 peppercorns
* ¼ oz mace
* ½ oz root ginger
* Pinch of cayenne pepper
* Onions, small whole
* Salt
* Water

Soak onions in brine made from 1 lb of salt to 1 gallon of water. Drain, peel and put into fresh brine. Drain again and pack into bottles and cover with spiced vinegar. Onions may be softened by boiling for 3 minutes a second time. Mix together and pour into bottles. Seal and store for a week before using.

'Tis breathed in vain!
J.P. 28 Mar

J.P.
Matins at St. Margarets.
27 March 1823

Ora pro nobis Margaretta!
J.P. 27 March 1823.

"By the waters of Ganges, we sat down
and wept; when we remembered thee
Oh Albion!"
James Prinsep.
27 March 1823

PICKLE FOR MEAT

* 48 units salt
* 8 units saltpetre
* 12 wine bottles water

Boil, skim and cool. Cover the meat with the pickle and rub over occasionally. It should be ready for use in 14 days but if taken out of the pickle and rubbed with salt and dried, it will keep for months in a dry climate. The pickle may be used again but must be boiled up and some more water added and ingredients added – a few spices and squeezed limes improve it for toughness.

TOMATO SAUCE FOR KEEPING

Excellent for camp work. To every 40 units of tomato pulp allow:

* 20 units vinegar
* 2 units salt
* 1 unit garlic
* ½ unit red chilli
* ¼ unit ground ginger
* Juice of 3 lemons

Boil all the ingredients until soft and pass through a sieve. Return to the pan and reduce till it is thick – it will keep for years.

Or add:

* 8 units sugar
* A season of mixed spices

Boil till quite a paste. Spread out to dry on plates in the sun. Cut up into strips. Wind them up and store in a dry place.

TOMATO SAUCE 2 (MRS KIDSTON)

* 12½ lb tomatoes
* 2 oz garlic
* 4 oz salt
* 1 teaspoon cayenne
* 4 oz onions
* 2 lb sugar
* 1 tablespoon cinnamon

Boil the above for 2 hours. Then strain. Then add from the chemist:

* *¼ g oil of cloves
* *1½ g acetic acid
* *½ g spirits of wine

*Get these three items from a chemist in three different bottles.

TOMATO SAUCE 3

* 12 lb tomatoes
* ¼ lb salt
* 1 oz peppercorns
* 2 oz whole allspice
* 4 lb sugar
* 4 large onions (whole)
* 1 oz cloves
* 2½ oz glacial acetic acid obtained from the chemist

Prick the skin on the whole tomatoes and stand in a bowl of boiling water for a minute or two. Remove and peel off the skin. Put in a pan with the sugar, salt, onions, tying spices in a muslin bag, adding a pinch of cayenne pepper or any other spice you wish. Boil for 3 hours. Remove the whole cooked onions, which have done their job, and the spice bag. Allow to cool to blood heat, then pour in the glacial acetic acid and stir thoroughly. Bottle. This sauce will not blow up, as some of my friends have discovered when using vinegar, and will keep indefinitely with cellophane or an ordinary lid.

GRAVY BROWNING

Put 2 tablespoons of sugar with 1 tablespoon of water in a pan. Put on a high heat but do not stir. Boil until the mixture has caramelised to a dark brown. Do not allow to burn. Pour in ½ breakfast cup of water and boil until the caramel has dissolved and is a dark syrup. When cold pour into a bottle and store. Use sparingly – a little goes a long way.

HARVEY'S SAUCE (MRS BEETON, *Directions for Cookery*, 1851)

* 1 pint vinegar
* 6 anchovies
* 2 heads of garlic
* 3 tablespoons soy sauce
* 3 tablespoons mushroom ketchup (recipe page 38)
* ¼ oz cayenne pepper
* Red food colouring

Dissolve the anchovies in the vinegar and then add the soy, mushroom ketchup and the cayenne pepper. Pour into a wide-mouthed jar. Divide and bruise the garlic and add to the liquid, along with a very small amount of red colouring. Close with the jar lid. Allow to infuse in the vinegar for 2 weeks, shaking every day. Strain and bottle in small sterilised bottles with airtight caps.

WALNUT KETCHUP (MRS BEETON)

* 2 pints vinegar
* 1 pint port wine
* 100 walnuts
* 20 shallots
* 4 oz anchovies
* ¼ oz mace
* ¼ oz cloves
* ¼ oz ginger
* ¼ oz whole black peppercorns
* 1 handful salt
* 1 small piece horseradish

The walnuts must be fresh and still green – soft enough for a pin to be pushed through. Bruise slightly and put into a jar with the salt and vinegar. Stand for 8 days, stirring every day. Drain the liquor from them and boil it with the above ingredients for 30 minutes. Pour into sterilised bottles with airtight caps.

MUSHROOM KETCHUP

- 16 pints in volume of freshly gathered, dry mushrooms
- 8 oz salt
- To each 2 pints of mushroom liquor allow:
- ½ oz allspice
- ½ oz ginger
- 2 blades mace, ground
- Brandy

Mix the salt with the mushrooms and allow to stand for a few hours, then break them up by hand. Put them in a cool place for 3 days, stirring occasionally and mashing well to extract as much juice as possible. Measure the quantity of liquor without straining and to each 2 pints allow the above proportion of spices. Put into a stone jar, cover tightly and put it in a saucepan of boiling water. Place over the heat and let it boil for 3 hours.

Have a clean saucepan ready and turn into it the contents of the jar and let everything simmer very quietly for 30 minutes. Pour into a jug and allow to cool till the next day. Then pour off into another jug and strain into sterilised bottles and do not squeeze the mushrooms. To each pint of ketchup add a few drops of brandy. Be careful not to shake the contents but leave all the sediment behind in the jug. Cork well.

ESSENCE OF PARSLEY

Wash it clean. Cut the roots into small pieces. Put the whole into a bottle and fill up with over-proof neutral spirit.

ESSENCE OF LEMONS

* 100 lemons
* 2 gallons of the very finest over-proof neutral spirit

Peel the lemons very thin and put them into a glass gallon jar, cover the parings with spirit. Squeeze the lemons, leave the juice to settle and strain it into a gallon jar and add 1 pint of spirit to preserve the juice, which will then be ready for use. The essence of lemon peel is delicious for flavouring jellies and makes the most delicious summer drink. (Perhaps it is 2 pints and not 2 gallons neutral spirit?)

Sauces and Stuffings

ANCHOVY SAUCE

* ½ pint melted butter
* 1 oz butter
* 4 anchovies
* Cayenne to taste
* Lemon juice (optional)

Bone the anchovies and pound in a mortar to a paste with 1 oz of butter. Stir into the melted butter, adding cayenne to taste. Simmer for 3 or 4 minutes and if liked, add a squeeze of lemon. Boil for one minute and serve hot.

Another way of preparing this is to stir in 1½ tablespoons of anchovy essence to ½ pint of melted butter and add seasoning to taste.

SAUCE PIQUANTE 1

* ½ pint of stock
* 1 oz butter
* 1 oz flour
* 1 teaspoon chopped parsley
* 1 teaspoon chopped gherkins
* 1 shallot
* 1 tablespoon vinegar (preferably tarragon)
* Gravy browning
* Salt and pepper

Wash, scrape and chop the shallot and put into a saucepan with the butter and vinegar. Put them on the fire and stir until the butter becomes quite clear and the vinegar reduces to half the quantity. Then add the flour, cook for 4 minutes and add the stock, stir well to prevent lumps. Add seasoning, a little caramel to colour, then add your gherkins and parsley. Bring to the boil, skim and serve. Only add salt if the stock has not had sufficient.

SAUCE PIQUANTE 2

Prepare mayonnaise adding to it a small quantity of French mustard (or ordinary), a few minced gherkins, a teaspoon of anchovy essence and a small quantity of minced chives or spring onions.

CUMBERLAND SAUCE

- 4 lemons
- 2 tablespoons Worcestershire sauce
- 2 tablespoons Harvey's sauce [see Mrs Beeton's recipe on page 36]
- 2 tablespoons King of Oudh sauce [or chutney]
- 1 tablespoon redcurrant jelly
- ½ pint water

Put the redcurrant jelly into a saucepan with ½ pint of boiling water, add the Harvey's sauce, juice of 4 lemons. Boil for 10 minutes to dissolve the redcurrant jelly. Then place in an earthenware basin and add the Worcestershire sauce and the King of Oudh sauce. Let the sauce get cold and cork and bottle. It improves by keeping. Serve cold.

MAYONNAISE SALAD DRESSING WITHOUT OIL

* 1 egg
* 3 tablespoons milk
* 2 tablespoons vinegar
* A walnut-sized lump of butter
* 1 teaspoon sugar
* 1 teaspoon dry mustard
* 1 teaspoon salt
* A dash of black pepper

Mix the vinegar, milk, mustard and salt. Beat the yolk and white of the egg together, then add the other ingredients, including the butter. This is best done in a large cup. Put the cup in a saucepan of boiling water and place on the fire stirring all the time. The moment it begins to thicken, remove the cup from saucepan and allow the contents to cool.

TARTARE SAUCE

As mayonnaise salad dressing without oil (above) but add:

* ½ oz chopped shallots
* ½ oz chopped gherkins
* 1 teaspoon chilli vinegar
* 1 teaspoon mustard

Mix well. This sauce is always served cold.

MAYONNAISE SAUCE (ABERFOYLE)

* 1 fresh egg, salt spoon of dry mustard

Beat in oil with a wooden spoon till quantity desired.

MAYONNAISE SAUCE 2

* 2 egg yolks
* 1 gill Lucca oil [Italian olive oil]
* Vinegar to taste

Put the egg yolks into a small basin and add the oil one drop at a time. When as thick as double cream add vinegar to taste. If the oil is added too rapidly the yolks curdle and no amount of stirring will bring them right again. But if you take 2 new yolks and use the curdled mixture as oil dropping it slowly on the fresh yolks as you ought to have done with the oil it will come together. Tarragon vinegar is an improvement.

SAUCE FOR SALADS

Mash yolks of 4 hard-boiled eggs and rub ½ teaspoon of pepper, 1 of salt and 1 tablespoon of sugar with 2 –3 teaspoons of prepared mustard. When well mixed add very slowly 4 tablespoons of oil, stirring all the while. When well mixed add 1 dessertspoon of Worcestershire sauce, 1½ tablespoons of white wine vinegar and a dessertspoon of tarragon vinegar.

If the sauce be required thicker increase the number of egg yolks or add a teaspoon of corn or other flour. Put the chosen flour into a cup and pour over it the quantity of vinegar prescribed above. Place the cup in a saucepan of boiling water over the fire and stir until the vinegar thickens to the desired consistency. Then blend it gradually with the preparation made first with the eggs, sugar, etc. until smooth and allow to cool before serving.

SAUCE FOR CUCUMBER SALAD

This sauce is also used occasionally to accompany lobster and prawn salads.

Slice into a soup plate 2 large onions and a couple of fresh chillies. Sprinkle with ground pepper and a little salt. Add 2 tablespoons vinegar and allow to stand for 2–3 hours before adding it to the sliced cucumbers.

AMERICAN SALAD DRESSING

* 2 tablespoons sugar
* 2 teaspoons cornflour
* ½ teaspoon mustard
* ½ teaspoon salt
* Small pinch bicarbonate of soda
* ½ cup milk
* ¼ cup vinegar
* 1 well-beaten egg
* Dessertspoon salad oil or butter

Mix well together the sugar, cornflour, mustard, salt, bicarbonate of soda. Add the milk, vinegar, egg and oil or butter. Put on the fire and stir until the dressing thickens. Do not boil. Allow to cool before serving. Delicious with cold salmon.

SALAD DRESSING WITH CONDENSED MILK

Mix to a smooth paste 1 tablespoon of sugar, ½ teaspoon of dry mustard, salt to taste, the yolk of a hard-boiled egg (this can be omitted) and a little vinegar. When very smooth, add alternately a little more vinegar then a little sweetened condensed milk until you have the desired amount and consistency remembering this dressing will thicken after standing an hour or two. This keeps in a cool place and will not separate.

SAUCE FOR ASPARAGUS

- 3 units water
- ¼ unit flour
- 1 unit salad oil
- ½ unit vinegar

Mix all the ingredients and put in a pan. Bring to the boil and set aside to cool. Pour over cold asparagus and serve.

ICED SAUCE FOR ASPARAGUS

* 3 units fresh butter, creamed
* 1 unit salad oil
* 1 unit tarragon vinegar
* ½ unit onion juice
* Whip in 3 units egg yolks
* Salt and pepper

The butter must be well warmed or the sauce will never get smooth. Salt and pepper. Allow to cool. Put asparagus on to a dish with the sauce in the middle set on ice.

EXCELLENT SAUCE FOR FISH

Wash and bone 2 anchovies and rub them in a mortar with ¼ lb butter and ½ teaspoon of flour. Put these into a small saucepan. Add to it the yolks of 3 eggs well beaten up, 2 tablespoons of tarragon vinegar, a small bunch of sweet herbs consisting of parsley, green onions, a bay leaf, a little salt, pepper and nutmeg. Stir these over the fire until the sauce is thick but be careful not to let it boil. Serve it up in a tureen.

MUSTARD SAUCE FOR FRESH HERRINGS

Cut off the heads of herrings, place with a cut-up onion, whole peppercorns in a saucepan. Add a little vinegar and as much water. Allow it to simmer at back of the stove for a long time. Make a pat of flour, mustard and butter. Drain liquid through a sieve and pour over the pat, thoroughly mix and allow to cook well for not less than 10 minutes. If the mixture becomes too thick add another piece of butter. This can be made hours before wanted and warmed through.

MUSTARD SAUCE 2

- 2 oz butter
- 1 dessertspoon sifted flour
- 1 dessertspoon mustard
- About ½ wineglass vinegar
- Salt
- Water

Put the mustard, flour and butter together adding a pinch of salt in a saucepan with a wineglass of boiling water. Simmer for a few minutes then add the vinegar. Serve in a small jug.

ONION SAUCE

Clean and boil 6–8 onions. Drain away the water. Fry an extra dessertspoon of finely chopped onions to a light brown colour in 4 oz butter. Mix in a tablespoon of sifted flour and 1 pint of milk, taking care to keep stirring to avoid lumps. Add a teaspoonful of salt and ¼ teaspoonful of pepper. Last of all add the boiled onions and in a few minutes the sauce will be ready.

BREAD SAUCE 1

Boil in a pint of water the crumb of a French roll or 6 oz of bread, a minced onion, some whole pepper. When the onion is cooked drain off the water, pick out the peppercorns and rub the bread through a sieve. Return it to the pan, add a gill of cream, a bit of butter the size of a walnut and some brown sugar. Heat and serve in a sauce tureen.

BREAD SAUCE 2

Soak 6 units of breadcrumbs in 6 units of thin white stock for an hour. Heat over the fire until like a panada, then thin with good béchamel.

BECHAMEL SAUCE

Flavour 5 units of milk with 1 carrot, 1 onion, some parsley, nutmeg, pepper and salt. Melt 2 units of butter in a saucepan. Stir in 1 unit of flour, strain hot milk to it and boil till thick enough. If wanted to mask chicken, etc. use ½ unit or more of cornflour as it sets better.

CREAM BECHAMEL

Add 8 units of yolks of eggs and lemon juice to above.

MAITRE D'HOTEL

2 units more butter than in béchamel recipe and add 2 units of chopped parsley, lemon juice.

SAUCE FOR WILD DUCK 1

Mix gradually in a basin 1 dessertspoon of lemon juice, 1 of powdered sugar, 1 of walnut ketchup, 1 of Harvey's sauce [see recipe page 36], 3 of port wine, 1 salt spoon of salt, ½ a salt spoon of cayenne. When all are well mixed, heat the sauce thoroughly and serve it in a tureen. It must be poured over the breast of the bird as soon as it is cut that it may mingle with the drawn gravy. No other gravy should be served with the duck.

SAUCE FOR WILD DUCK 2

* Juice of 1 lemon
* 2 tablespoons port wine
* ½ tablespoon onion juice
* 2 tablespoons gravy
* Pepper and salt

Mix all the above and serve hot.

FRESH TOMATO GRAVY SAUCE FOR MADE DISHES

Take 40 tomatoes (halved), some soup herbs and salt. Boil them in a little stock, strain, replace on the fire and thicken with the addition of more or less a dessertspoon of arrowroot or corn or any other flour, to obtain the required consistency. Finally add a teaspoonful of good English vinegar.

PARSLEY SAUCE

Wash and chop some fresh parsley and put it into a tureen with a tablespoon of chopped capers and a teaspoonful of English vinegar. Fry a dessertspoon of chopped onions in 4 oz of butter until light brown. Add a cupful of good white stock and thicken with a crumb of stale bread finely grated, a teaspoonful of salt and a little pepper. Pour it over the parsley and capers and mix well.

ORANGE SYRUP

When using 1 heaped dessertspoon of light ingredients like flour = ½ oz. When using a level dessertspoon of heavy ingredients like sugar, currants, etc. = ½ oz.

* 4 oranges
* 1 lemon
* 2½ lb sugar
* 1½ pints boiling water
* ½ oz citric acid
* ½ oz tartaric acid
* ½ oz Epsom salts

Grate zest of lemon and oranges and squeeze juice (makes ½ pint). Put in a basin with sugar and crystals. Pour the boiling water over and after stirring well leave overnight. Strain and bottle. Dilute to taste.

SWEET SAUCE

* 1 unit cornflour
* 2 units sugar
* 5 units sherry
* 1 unit lemon juice
* 1 unit butter
* 10 units water

Add the cold water to the other ingredients, stir and bring to the boil. Simmer for a minute or two until thick and serve.

BRANDY SAUCE FOR PLUM PUDDING

* ¼ lb butter
* ¼ lb caster sugar
* Good brandy and sherry

Partially melt the butter and heat up with the sugar till it looks like whipped cream. Then stir in gradually a wineglass of brandy and ½–¾ glass of sherry (sherry size). To be served with hot plum pudding.

OATMEAL AND BACON STUFFING

For breast of lamb or boned leg of mutton.

- 2 tablespoons chopped, crispy fried bacon
- 1½ gills rolled oats
- ½ gill soft breadcrumbs
- 1 oz margarine or butter
- ½ gill chopped onions
- ½ teaspoonful mixed herbs
- A good pinch of salt
- A pinch of pepper
- 1 tablespoon water

Fry the chopped onions in the bacon fat and margarine till golden brown. Add all the dry ingredients and mix well. Lastly, add the water.

STUFFING FOR ROAST DUCK 1

Shred enough of the heart of a cabbage as will suffice for stuffing. It will reduce with cooking. Wash and dry thoroughly. Add a teaspoon of ground pepper, 1 of salt, 3 cloves of garlic and 4 oz butter. Mix together and insert in duck, baking or roasting as you please.

STUFFING FOR DUCK OR GOOSE 2

* 2 units pulped apples
* 1 unit pulped onions
* Sage to flavour
* 6 units potatoes
* 2 units egg to bind

GRAVY BALLS

* 4 oz shredded suet
* 4 oz flour
* ½ teaspoon baking powder
* 4 oz fine oatmeal
* Salt and pepper
* Water to mix

Mix together dry ingredients, then add sufficient water to make a firm dough. Flour the hands and form the dough into small balls. Have ready the gravy [recipe right] brought to the boil. Drop in the balls one by one and boil for 5 minutes, then cover over, reduce the heat and allow to simmer gently for about 30 minutes. Look at it from time to time and, if necessary, add more liquid. See that the gravy doesn't simmer away which must be boiling when added. Serve in a bowl with gravy.

GRAVY

- 2 oz ghee
- 2 breakfast cups water
- 4 teaspoons ground onions
- 1 teaspoon turmeric
- 1 teaspoon chillies
- ½ teaspoon dried ginger
- ¼ teaspoon ground garlic
- ½ teaspoon roasted coriander (if desired)

Heat the ghee in a pan and add all the ground condiments, stirring until quite brown. Add the water and allow to simmer until it has thickened and makes a nice brown gravy.

Soups

SOUP MAIGRE

* 1½ pints water
* 1 turnip
* 1 carrot
* 1 stick of celery
* 3 potatoes
* 1 dessertspoon flour
* ½ pint milk
* Salt to taste

Wash, peel and chop the vegetables. Melt a tablespoon of good beef dripping in a pan and when hot, tip in the vegetables and salt. Stir and allow them to sweat in the fat but without browning. Add the water, bring to the boil and simmer for an hour until tender. Pass through a sieve and return to the pan. Add the milk. Blend the flour in a little cold water and add to the soup, stirring until it is thickened. Simmer for 5 minutes and serve with croutons of fried bread.

MESS OF POTTAGE

- ½ a small cabbage or an equal quantity of Swiss chard
- 1 onion
- 1 small turnip
- 1 large potato
- ½ cup lentils (or split peas)
- ½ cup pearl barley
- Salt and pepper to taste

Put the split peas or lentils and the pearl barley to soak for ½ hour in a bowl of cold water. Remove the central core and tough outer leaves of the cabbage and discard. Shred the remaining cabbage (or Swiss chard) finely. Heat some good dripping in a pan and fry for a few minutes, stirring all the while. Add the onion, turnip and potato (all peeled and finely chopped into small dice). Add the soaked split peas or lentils and the pearl barley. Cover well with water and bring to the boil. Reduce the heat and continue cooking gently for 1½ hours, taking care it does not burn. Season with salt and pepper to taste. Serve with a sprinkling of chopped parsley.

POTAGE BONNE FEMME 1

This soup should have shredded leaves of spinach added at the end. They will wilt in the hot broth. Gather together any amount and kind of beans, lettuce, onion, carrots, cucumber that are to hand. Peel where necessary and chop finely. Melt a tablespoon of butter in a saucepan and add all the vegetables. Sweat for five minutes, stirring every now and then. Add 1 pint of water and bring to the boil, then reduce heat and simmer until the vegetables are cooked (about 15 minutes). Push through a sieve. In a separate saucepan, blend 1 cupful of cream with the yolk of an egg. Slowly pour the hot soup on to the cream and egg, stirring so that the egg doesn't curdle. Return to the heat and continue cooking for a further 2–3 minutes. Do not boil. Season with salt and pepper and serve at once.

POTAGE BONNE FEMME 2

* ½ lettuce
* ½ cucumber
* 1 small/medium onion
* 1 pint milk
* 1 oz butter
* Thickening of yolks of 2 eggs or 2 teaspoons flour
* Salt and pepper to taste

Shred the vegetables and cook in milk and butter till tender. Put through a sieve and thicken. Season and serve.

MULLIGATAWNY SOUP

* 4 oz desiccated coconut
* 2 pints of concentrated stock
* 2 oz ghee
* 4 oz chopped onions
* 2 oz lentils
* 1 tablespoon curry powder
* Salt
* 4 bay leaves
* 1 small chicken
* Water

Make coconut milk by steeping the desiccated coconut in a bowl with ½ pint of boiling water. Leave to become quite cold and rub through a fine sieve to extract the milk. Throw out the coconut pulp.

Cut up the chicken into pieces. Heat the ghee in a saucepan and fry the onions until nice and brown, add the curry powder and fry for a further 2–3 minutes. Add the chicken pieces and fry, stirring constantly until brown all over. Season with salt. Pour in the coconut milk and simmer for 10 minutes until the chicken is cooked and tender.

Pick out some nice pieces of cooked breast as a garnish and break up the remainder to strengthen the soup. Heat the stock and add the chicken, onion and curry mixture, the lentils and bay leaves. Boil gently for 2 hours until the lentils are dissolved and the soup quite thick.

Strain the soup before serving. Add the reserved pieces of chicken. Serve with a bowl of plain boiled rice and sliced lemon so that the juice may be added if desired to each bowl.

TOMATO PULP SOUP

- 4 lb tomatoes
- 1 teaspoonful salt
- 2 onions
- Peppercorns
- A little thyme
- 2 quarts water

Put all ingredients into a large saucepan.

KIDNEY SOUP

Cut up an ox kidney very small and flour well. Put a dessertspoonful of butter in a pan and brown a little. Fry kidney until brown, then put in saucepan with about 1½ pints of water with carrot and turnip and any other vegetables well cut up and stew gently for some time until well cooked. If liked, thicken a little and flavour with vinegar and sauce.

MIXED VEGETABLE SOUP

* 3 pints of stock
* 1 whole cabbage
* 1 lb potatoes
* ¼ lb rice
* 1 teaspoonful salt
* ½ teaspoonful ground pepper
* 2 oz grated cheese

Cut the cabbage in half and then into quarters removing the hard, central core. Peel the potatoes and cut into quarters. Put the vegetables in a saucepan and cover with stock, add salt and pepper. When the potatoes are cooked, add the rice which has been thoroughly washed. When the rice has boiled to a mash, the soup is ready. Stir in the grated cheese and serve immediately.

PUMPKIN SOUP WITH CROUTONS

* 1 lb ripe pumpkin (butternut or any sweet squash)
* 1½ pints of stock
* 1 teaspoonful salt
* 1 salt spoonful ground pepper
* Small bunch of herbs
* For the croutons: 1 slice bread and 1 tablespoon ghee

Remove the peel and seeds from the pumpkin and cut into small pieces. Put it into a saucepan and add the stock and herbs, bring to the boil and simmer till tender. Remove the herbs and rub the pumpkin through a sieve. Add salt and pepper and once boiled again it is ready to serve. A little milk may be added.

To make the croutons: remove the crust and cut into small squares. Fry in boiling ghee till crisp and brown. Drain on paper and serve with the soup.

EGG SOUP

- ½ pint of good strong chicken stock
- 2 oz dried vermicelli
- 2 oz butter
- 2 eggs
- ½ teaspoonful ground pepper
- Salt

Boil the stock, add salt and pepper and add the vermicelli. Simmer until tender. Put the butter in a basin over a pan of hot water and beat it to a cream. Add the eggs to the butter and beat well together until quite smooth. Put the egg and butter mixture into a soup tureen and pour the boiling soup on to them, stir and serve at once.

Fish

GREAT-UNCLE ALICK'S FISH PIE (SIR ALEXANDER CAMPBELL, 4TH BARONET OF BARCALDINE)

* 2 fillets fish
* 8 oz new potatoes, washed with their skins left on, sliced to about the thickness of a pound coin
* 2 medium onions, peeled and finely chopped
* 1 clove of garlic, peeled and finely chopped
* ½–¾ teaspoon fennel seeds (optional)
* Scant ¼ teaspoon dried chilli flakes
* Salt and pepper
* 2 tablespoons olive oil
* 1 glass white wine
* 1 lemon

Lay the potato slices on to the bottom of a buttered dish followed by the onions. Add garlic, fennel seeds and chilli. Season and drizzle over some good olive oil. Bake for 15–20 minutes until the potatoes are almost done. Remove from the oven and add the fish fillets. Pour in the wine and add sliced lemon and a little more olive oil. Bake a further 15 minutes. Serve immediately.

KEDGEREE OF FISH

Take 6 units of boiled rice and flaked fish, some pepper, salt and 2 units of hard-boiled egg, chopped fine. Heat together over a fire, moistening slightly with a little butter or cream, or a little raw egg.

PRAWN CUTLETS

* 2 oz butter
* ½ teaspoonful each of salt and pepper
* 1 teaspoon herbs

Wash and shell as many prawns as required, remove heads but leave the tails. Slit them down the centre and sprinkle with pepper and salt and some finely chopped herbs. Brush them over with egg and breadcrumbs and then fry in the butter over a moderate fire a rich brown.

PRAWN CURRY

Tomatoes and cucumbers make a nice addition to this curry. Core and quarter the tomatoes, cut the cucumber into 4 pieces, lengthways. Whichever vegetable is used, it should be added after the prawns are browned, and no water added.

* ½ lb prawns
* 3 oz ghee
* 1 dessertspoon curry powder
* ½ teaspoonful salt
* 2 oz onions, sliced
* Water

Melt the ghee in a pan and fry the onions until brown, then add the curry powder, stir well. Add the prawns and keep stirring them on a brisk fire until they are also well browned. Add the salt and ¼ pint of hot water. Cover the pan and simmer for 10 minutes when the curry will be ready to serve.

SARDINE ROLLS

* ½ lb flaky pastry
* 1 tin sardines
* Juice of ½ lemon

Mash sardines with lemon juice and pepper. Spread over pastry rolled very thin. Roll up into rolls 1 inch thick and cut into inch lengths. Bake in quick oven.

OR:

Have as many required slices of thin fresh bread and butter. Cut off crust. In each slice roll a sardine, tail removed. Put in a good oven and bake till crisp and brown.

SMOKED FISH SAVOURY

Make a stiff white sauce. Add cooked, flaked smoked fish and seasoning. Spread on thin white bread and butter. Roll up and bake light brown in oven.

OYSTER COCKTAIL (FOR 4 GLASSES)

* Beard and cut up oysters very small
* 2 tablespoons tomato ketchup
* 2 tablespoons vinegar
* 2 tablespoons oyster liquid
* 2 teaspoons Worcestershire sauce
* Few drops lemon juice

Mix liquid ingredients and add chopped oysters. Put in glasses and just before serving top with finely chopped celery and grated horseradish and a small spoonful of whipped cream.

FILLETS OF FISH A LA COLBERT

* Filleted fish
* Salt and pepper
* Lemon juice
* Onion juice
* White sauce

Butter a pie or 'eared' dish. Lay the fillets in layers seasoning each layer with a little onion juice and a drop of lemon juice. Pour the white sauce over and bake till brown.

FISH RAGOUT

Peel, chop and drain 5 small tomatoes and put them in a saucepan with 1 small, chopped onion, a tablespoon of Worcestershire sauce and 2 tablespoons of olive oil.

Season with salt and pepper and cook for 20 minutes, stirring regularly. Then add 2 lb of firm, white fish, skin removed and cut in pieces. Cover closely and simmer for 25 minutes. Serve with plain boiled rice.

PICKLED FISH

- Herrings, mackerel or sprats
- 1 gill vinegar
- 1 bay leaf
- Blade mace
- Salt and peppercorns

Place all the ingredients in a baking dish and cover tightly. Bake in a very slow oven until the fish is cooked through. Allow to cool before serving with thinly sliced brown bread and butter.

FISH CURRY

* 1 lb cooked fish, flaked into pieces (any skin and bones removed)
* 2 oz sliced onions
* 2 oz butter
* ½ teaspoonful powdered turmeric
* Small piece of fresh ginger
* 1 dessertspoon sliced green chillies
* 1 tablespoon vinegar
* ½ lb desiccated coconut
* Bay leaf
* A salt spoon of salt

Put the coconut into a basin and cover with boiling water. Let it stand for an hour, then strain through a muslin or fine sieve, throwing away the pulp.

Poach the fish either in milk or water, or a mixture of both, with a bay leaf, in a baking dish in a hot oven for about 15 minutes.

Pound the ginger in a mortar with a little water to make a paste.

Heat the butter in a pan and fry the onions to a rich brown. Add the turmeric, ginger, chillies, salt, coconut milk, the flaked fish and lastly the vinegar. Stir carefully and as soon as the sauce thickens the curry is ready. Serve with boiled rice.

FRIED SPRATS

Sprinkle a frying pan with salt. Warm it through and throw your sprats in. Shake the pan to prevent the fish burning. No fat required for frying.

BAKED SPRATS

Take a small pie dish, cover the bottom with breadcrumbs and chopped herbs, put a layer of sprats, then another of breadcrumbs and so on until the dish is full. Add one gill of water or stock and cover dish with breadcrumbs or mashed potato. Put a few pieces of butter or dripping on top. To clean sprats, wipe the fish and cook it whole. It is a clean little fish and it requires nothing further.

PLAIN BAKED FISH

- 1 small salmon trout, brown trout or bream
- 1 cup breadcrumbs
- 1 unit chopped parsley
- 1 unit grated onion
- Lemon juice
- Salt and pepper to taste

Wash the fish and pat dry. Mix all the other ingredients together and fill the cavity with the stuffing mixture. Secure by tying string around the fish. Wrap it in some buttered greaseproof paper and lay on an oven dish. Bake in a hot oven for 15–20 minutes.

FISH BALLS

Place a whole (gutted and washed) salmon trout in a pan with salted boiling water until cooked. Lift the skin off the cooked fish. Mix the fish with an equal quantity of mashed potato seasoned well with salt and pepper. Bind with a beaten egg. Shape into flat, round cakes and cover in dried breadcrumbs. Leave in a cool place an hour before cooking. Fry in fat to a golden brown, on both sides. Serve with tomatoes.

SARDINE SAVOURIES

- 1 tin sardines
- 1½ oz butter
- 1 teaspoonful anchovy sauce
- 1 teaspoonful Worcestershire sauce
- 1 dessertspoon flour
- Scant ½ pint boiling water
- Pinch of cayenne
- Lemon juice

Fry some rounds of stale bread in deep, boiling fat until golden brown. Remove and drain well on kitchen paper and put to one side, keeping warm.

Drain the oil from the sardines and mash them. Spread the paste on to the croutons. Melt the butter in a saucepan, add the flour stirring well to avoid any lumps and add the savoury sauces and a pinch of cayenne. Then add the boiling water and a good squeeze of lemon juice, stirring continuously. Cook for five minutes. Spoon over the prepared croutons and serve at once.

BOUILLABAISSE

Cannot be made to rule: take 1, 2, or 3 onions according to quantity required, 1 clove garlic, handful of parsley, pepper, lemon juice, spice salt (recipe page 27), saffron.

Put 10 units of water and 2 units oil in a pan, add all the above ingredients and as many different kinds of fish as you can get hold of in equal proportions. Put over a fierce fire and the bouillabaisse is done in ¼ hour.

BAKED AND STUFFED FISH

* 1 haddock
* 2 units breadcrumbs
* Chopped parsley
* 1 teaspoonful chopped herbs
* Blade mace
* 2 oz suet
* 1 egg

Make a stuffing as for veal or, if for a maigre dish, replace the suet with another egg and more breadcrumbs. Clean the fish well, stuff the belly with the mixture and sew it up. Take a trussing needle with a strong twine and pass it through the eye sockets and the crest part of the back near the tail and pull the fish into a letter 's'.

Egg and brown breadcrumb, place on a greased baking sheet, baste well and bake for ½ hour.

LOBSTER SALAD IN ASPIC

Pour the liquid aspic jelly into a border mould to the depth of ½ inch and let it set. Have ready the meat of the lobster cut into small pieces, lay it in a circle in the mould but not touching the sides. When the top of the mould is reached fill up with more aspic jelly and put it away to set. Clean a lettuce and break it up. When the mould is set, turn out the jelly and fill in the centre with the lettuce over which pour plenty of mayonnaise sauce. Garnish with cucumber and hard-boiled eggs. Keep in a cool place till ready to serve.

Meat and Poultry

GALANTINE OF BEEF

* 6 oz lean beef
* 6 oz ham
* 2 oz breadcrumbs
* 1 egg
* Salt and pepper

Mince the beef and ham as finely as possible. Add the breadcrumbs and egg and seasoning and mix very well. Form into a rather flat roll, wrap in a cloth and steam for 2 hours. When cold the roll should be glazed with a little gelatine just melted into a little water and made dark brown colour.

SPICED BEEF

Make a pickle salt of:

* 48 units salt
* 3 units each of saltpetre and sugar
* Savoury herbs
* 2 cloves garlic
* ½ unit each of cloves, mace and ground peppercorns

Rub into a piece of brisket of beef for 8 days morning and evening for ¼ hour. Remove the bones, roll and stew gently till done. Remove and put under a heavy weight. When cold, trim and glaze.

HINDU'S BEEF

Salt in pickle [recipe page 32] for 3 days, then rub with spices as follows: 1 unit each of cloves, cinnamon, cardamoms, allspice, mace and 2 units of black pepper. Continue rubbing morning and evening for 8 days. Wash off spices. Lay in a flat earthenware dish with suet in thin slices under and over. Cover with a flour and water crust and bake.

BEEF ROLL

- 1 lb beef steak, or any lean part, raw
- ½ lb breadcrumbs
- 2 eggs (more if Indian)
- A little nutmeg and salt and pepper

Mince finely, mix well together, add ingredients with the eggs well beaten. Make into the shape of a large, fat sausage. Tie firmly in a cloth to boil for 4 hours. Glaze when cold.

POTTED MEAT

* 1 lb thick skirt steak
* 1 teaspoonful mace
* Salt and pepper to taste
* ¼ lb butter
* ½ teaspoonful nutmeg
* 2 tablespoons anchovy sauce

Cut steak up roughly, add half the butter and put with all the other ingredients into a double boiler. Cook for 2 hours.

Put through the mincer twice. Leave enough room to put melted butter on top to keep.

IMITATION PATE DE FOIE GRAS

Put 16 units of calf's liver with 8 units of bacon into a pan and cover with tepid water. Add ½ teaspoonful of salt and bake till very tender for 1–1½ hours. Strain and reserve the liquor. Pass the cooked liver and bacon through a mincer twice, then moisten with 2 units of melted butter. Work into a paste and add ¼ teaspoonful pepper, a pinch of cayenne, ¼ teaspoonful grated nutmeg, 1½ teaspoons dry mustard and ½ teaspoon salt.

Pack into jars and cover with more melted butter. Use for sandwiches or hot toast for afternoon tea. Use the reserved liquor for soup.

MEAT CURRY

For curry to be good, it must take 2 hours at least to make.

* 1 unit ghee
* 1 unit curry powder
* 4 units peeled and sliced onions
* 1 teaspoonful salt
* ½ lb beef, mutton, lamb or pork
* Water

Cut beef into 1 inch squares. All other meat may be cut in the same way in neat pieces. Heat ghee in a saucepan and fry half the onions till brown. Add curry powder and fry together for 3 or 4 minutes. Add salt and ¼ pint of hot water, stir well, then add another ¼ pint of hot water and let the whole boil fast without stirring for a few minutes, or until it begins to stick on the bottom of the pan. Do not let it burn. Add ½ pint more hot water, stir and add meat and the rest of the onions. Stir well and simmer till meat is tender and fully cooked. The addition of ¼ pint of cold milk added at the same time as the meat is an improvement – the water proportionately reduced. For beef curry add sprigs of fennel. Curries may be varied by the addition of vegetables.

MUTTON

Boil a leg of mutton for ½ hour before baking it. It will not only be more juicy and tender but will save shrinkage.

MEAT CURRY WITH FRUIT

* 1 medium onion per person
* 1 tablespoon curry powder to 1 lb meat (chicken, mutton/lamb or beef)
* ¼ pint coconut milk for 2 people (recipe page 29)
* Fruit for flavouring: sultanas, apples, mangoes
* Ghee
* ¼ pint of stock or water per person

Brown the onions in boiling grease. Remove and add to the grease the curry powder, stir and add the coconut milk and fruit. Brown for 15 minutes stirring diligently. Simmer the meat in stock or water for 15 minutes. Remove the meat from the stock and fry in a separate pan. Brown for 15 minutes. Mix in the onion and curry mixture and add stock as required for a wet or dry curry.

PISH-PASH

* 1½ lb mutton (loin, neck or scrag)
* ½ lb rice
* Salt to taste
* A few whole cloves, peppercorns and a stick of cinnamon

Cut the mutton into chops and boil in enough water to cover well. Bring to the boil, remove any scum and drain in a colander. Replace the chops in the pan with fresh water and bring to the boil. When the meat is half cooked (after approximately 15–20 minutes), add the rice, salt and spices and more water if necessary. Stir to mix well. When the rice is cooked the dish is ready – it should have the consistency of mash without there being a separate broth.

BRAIN PATTIES

* 1 lb sheep's brains
* 1 cup flour
* 1 teaspoonful baking powder
* 1 egg
* Salt
* 1 tablespoon chopped parsley
* Enough cold water to make into a stiff batter
* 2 oz ghee

Put 1 lb sheep's brains into a pan with water, bring to the boil and simmer gently for 10 minutes. Drain, skim and stir mix into the batter. Fry in very hot ghee to a nice golden brown. Delicious for lunch with mashed potatoes.

CURRIED MEATBALLS

Any raw or cooked meat can be used up in this manner.

* ½ lb meat (raw or cooked)
* ¼ lb onions, peeled and chopped
* 1 unit chopped parsley
* 2 oz breadcrumbs
* 2 oz ghee
* 1 tablespoon curry powder
* 1 teaspoonful salt
* ¼ pint buttermilk or milk
* 1 egg
* Water

Prepare meat by removing gristle and stringy parts and pound in a mortar or pass through a mincer two or three times. Season well with pepper and salt, the chopped parsley and a teaspoonful of the chopped onions. Mix with the breadcrumbs and egg to bind it. Divide into 12 balls and dredge them with flour to prevent sticking. Stand in a soup plate with the buttermilk (or milk) and soak for quarter of a hour or longer.

Heat the ghee and fry half the remaining onions till brown, add the curry powder and fry together 3–4 minutes, stirring all the while. Add ¼ pint of hot water, stir and let it boil a few minutes without further stirring. Add another ¼ pint of hot water, salt and the remainder of the onions and stir. Place the meatballs in the gravy and any of the milk which has not been absorbed. Cover with a lid and let it simmer for 1 hour. The meatballs should remain in one piece.

MEAT ROASTED IN A SAUCEPAN

Meat cooked in a pan on the fire retains its juices and is very tender. Any type of meat can be cooked in this manner as well as poultry. Potatoes roasted with the meat are very nice and put them in ¾ hour before the end of cooking the meat.

Put 2 oz butter or good dripping in a pan large enough to take the piece of meat or chicken. Dredge the meat with salt, pepper and flour rubbing in all over. Brown the meat in the fat. No water is needed if the meat is fat but poultry and lean meat will need extra butter and ¼ pint of hot water added when the meat is browned.

Put on the cover and shake the pan constantly to prevent burning. Simmer quietly, basting and moving it about frequently in the pan till cooked thoroughly. Make gravy in normal way. I would suggest draining off any excess fat, stir a tablespoon of flour into the juices before adding some vegetable stock or boiling water. Bring to the boil and simmer for a minute or two to thicken. There will be no need for further seasoning.

BAKED STEAK

Mix together 1 teaspoon sugar, 1 teaspoon of flour and pinch of bicarbonate. Pepper and salt to taste and 1 dessertspoon of vinegar. Rub this mixture well into 1 lb steak with the back of a spoon and put into a covered casserole. Add a little stock or water.

BREADED CUTLETS

* 1-2 cutlets per person
* 1 inch piece of fresh, root ginger
* 1 teaspoonful onion juice
* Fresh breadcrumbs
* Flour
* 1 egg, beaten
* Salt and pepper

Beat the cutlets flat with a rolling pin and season with salt and pepper. Peel the ginger and pound in a mortar with a little water to extract the juice. Make a teaspoonful of onion juice by scraping an onion with a spoon. Rub the cutlets all over with a mixture of a teaspoonful of the ginger juice and the onion juice. Let the meat stand for an hour or longer.

When ready to cook, dredge the cutlets in flour, then dip into beaten egg and cover with fresh breadcrumbs. Fry in hot fat and serve. A gravy can be made by adding a little hot water and a heaped tablespoon of more fresh breadcrumbs into the pan. Stir well for a minute or two and add enough hot water to make a good, thick gravy.

DEVIL MEAT

This dish is normally prepared with raw chicken but it is very suitable for cooked poultry and meats, which should be first cut into slices.

* 2 oz ghee
* 1 unit chutney
* 1 unit Worcestershire sauce
* 1 teaspoonful powdered chillies
* 1 teaspoonful made mustard
* 2 tablespoons vinegar
* 1 teaspoonful salt
* 2 oz sliced onions
* Water

Fry the onions in the ghee until brown and add all the other condiments, mixing well. Add the pieces of raw chicken and fry till brown. If using cooked meat, add about ¼ pint of hot water at the same time. Stir and cover and simmer until the chicken is tender and the water absorbed.

CROQUETTES

* ¾ lb of any lean cooked meat
* 1 oz onions
* 2 oz fresh breadcrumbs
* Pinch of chopped parsley
* 2 oz ghee
* 2 eggs
* 1 teaspoonful salt
* ½ teaspoonful pepper

Pound the meat in a mortar or pass through a mincer 2 or 3 times. Add the breadcrumbs, onions, parsley, salt and pepper and pound well, then work in the yolk of 1 egg and the whites of both, beaten separately to a stiff snow.

Shape the mixture into croquettes, dip in the remaining beaten egg yolk and dredge with flour. Heat the ghee in a pan and fry as quickly as possible to a nice brown. Fry some sprigs of parsley or mint as a garnish.

JIMMY

Cut any cold meat (white meat of the chicken is best) into small pieces. Put a small lump of butter in a frying pan and when melted, add a tablespoon or more of milk. Add the meat, salt and pepper and a few slices of onion and green chilli. Stir. Break over the meat one or more eggs according to the quantity of meat. Stir altogether and as soon as the eggs are set, turn out and serve like scrambled eggs.

COOKED MEAT CURRY

* ¼ lb cooked meat
* ¼ lb onions
* 2 oz butter
* 1 dessertspoon curry powder
* ½ teaspoonful salt
* ½ teaspoonful powdered chillies or 1 fresh green chilli
* Splash of Worcestershire sauce
* Water

Heat butter in a pan and fry onions till brown. Add curry powder, chillies, meat and salt with 1 unit of hot water – add more if necessary. Fry all well together till rich, dark brown.

CHINA HASH

A little spoon of curry powder is an improvement.

* 40 units raw minced mutton
* 20 units shredded lettuce
* 20 units peas
* 10 units carrots and turnips mixed
* 5 units water
* 2 units butter
* Salt and pepper

Put all together, stir till hot, then cover and simmer for 2 hours. Serve with rice.

ch w
ry would her get
than the at tion of is c ed to the
N L y, by a sm
r sk, they may get au t They
should has the n est L y Off
and t by pur ing n a S they
may cure w they and not
fail to make the go, and them, (if
their Deity) an ly
2 Grand Prizes of £30,000
And FIFTY OTHER CAPITALS.

MINAR at GOUR

DUM
SPIRO
SPERO

C Hambro
Indian temple +
village Hills

One Gun Battery Corfu

PORK CURRY

Do not use an iron pan to prepare this dish.

* 1 lb loin of pork cut into chops
* ¼ lb butter
* ¼ pint vinegar
* 1 dessertspoon curry powder
* Salt to taste
* 2 bay leaves

Divide each chop in two across the bone. Place in a china basin with the curry powder and salt. Mix well and add the vinegar, stirring thoroughly. Lastly, add the butter, not melted but broken into pieces, and the bay leaves. Mix well and leave in a cool place for 2 days.

Put in an enamel saucepan without any water and simmer quietly, stirring constantly until it is a brown colour and the meat is cooked. Do not let it burn. Serve with boiled rice.

HAM TO BOIL

English ham is worth taking a little trouble. If fresh, it is not necessary to soak more than 1 hour, just to remove dirt, etc. Let it be well washed and rubbed all over with vinegar and pepper and washed again. Put 1 bottle of country vinegar, ½ bottle of white wine, 4 carrots, some thyme, peppercorns, mace and ½ lb beef suet with enough warm water to cover the ham. Boil for 10 minutes and put the ham in it and let it cook. Then boil about ½ hour for each lb of ham and let the whole get cold together.

Hams are also excellent baked like Hunter's Beef, with ½ bottle of wine added to the suet. Helen [Shaw] puts a good dollop of treacle when ham has almost finished boiling – say, last ½ hour of cooking.

RABBIT PIE

Line a dish with streaky bacon. Cut up rabbit in neat joints and put in a dish with a whole pepper and a bouquet of herbs on top of last layer of bacon. Season. Pour in 2 glasses of sherry and 1 glass of brandy. Cover with a lid of thick paste made from flour and water. Cook in very slow oven for 1–1½ hours. Remove paste and herbs. Serve hot.

CHICKEN DUMPODE

1 boned chicken. Make a forcemeat with boiled rice (as for pilau) and fresh herbs, onions and hard-boiled eggs. Stuff the chicken with this and braise in a medium oven.

BEEF OR MUTTON BAKED WITH POTATOES

* Potatoes (1 large one per person)
* 1 egg, beaten
* ¼ pint milk
* Onion
* Slices of raw beef or mutton chops
* Salt and pepper to taste

Quantities depend on how many are to be served, and adjust accordingly.

Boil the potatoes in their jackets. When cooked, peel and pound them with 1 or 2 small raw onions, which have been peeled and chopped finely.

Add some milk, the egg, salt and pepper, beating thoroughly. Season slices of beef or mutton chops with salt and pepper. Butter a pie dish and put in a thick layer of potato mash – this should have the consistency of very thick batter. Add a layer of meat, then potato and so on ending with potatoes. Bake in a brisk oven for 1 hour until bubbling and golden brown.

PILAU (OR PELLOW) 1

* A good-sized chicken
* ½ lb rice, washed
* 2 oz ghee
* 1 onion
* 6 almonds, blanched and sliced
* 2 oz sultanas or raisins
* 1 teaspoonful salt
* 3 cardamoms
* 4 cloves
* 1 blade mace
* 2 sticks of cinnamon
* 12 peppercorns
* Water

Clean and truss the chicken and boil in only as much water as is necessary, with the onion and half the salt.

When tender, remove from the fire and set aside. Strain the stock and bring it back to the boil.

Melt the ghee in a large pan and fry the rice until golden, add the remaining salt and spices and then enough of the stock to cover the rice. Cover the pan and let the rice boil but do not let it burn. Continue adding more hot stock as it is absorbed until the rice is fully cooked without turning into a mash.

Add the almonds and raisins and reduce the heat, leaving the pan covered. Shake from time to time to prevent the rice from sticking. In a few minutes it will be dry.

To serve, place the chicken in a dish and pile the rice over and around it.

PILAU 2

Slice 6 large onions and 2 green mangoes and fry in 2 units of butter and set aside. Truss a chicken as for boiling and fry it in 2 units of butter and put into the stew pan. Cover with water and stew gently. When half done, remove and finish cooking as for roast chicken.

Wash 4 units of rice and fry in butter, then boil in the chicken stock. Add a little butter and sultanas, almonds, cloves, etc. and let it dry. Serve round the chicken with the stock reduced as gravy and a decoration of hard-boiled eggs.

MUTTON PILAU

Substitute mutton for chicken.

CHICKEN CURRY 1

* 1 small chicken
* 2 oz ghee
* 4 oz onions, chopped
* 4 oz desiccated coconut
* 1 tablespoon curry powder
* 1 teaspoonful salt
* Pinch of powdered cloves
* Pinch of powdered cinnamon
* 3 cardamoms

Cut the chicken into pieces. Soak the desiccated coconut in a pint of hot water for an hour or longer, then rub through a sieve. The extract is to be used, and discard the pulp.

Heat the ghee and fry the curry powder, ground spices and onions together to a good brown colour. Add the chicken and fry until brown. Lastly, add the salt and coconut milk – this should be warmed first – and the cardamoms. Stir, then cover and simmer quietly until the chicken is tender. There should be about ½ pint of thick gravy.

CHICKEN CURRY 2

- 1 chicken
- 2 oz butter
- 2 breakfast cups water
- ½ teaspoonful salt
- 4 teaspoons ground onions
- 1 teaspoon each of ground turmeric and chillies
- ½ teaspoon ground ginger
- ¼ teaspoon ground garlic
- ½ teaspoon ground coriander seed if it suits your taste. These should be roasted before being ground

Divide the chicken into many pieces. Melt the butter and add all the condiments stirring until brown. Add the chicken and salt and fry to a light brown colour. Add the water and allow to simmer over a slow fire until the chicken is quite tender and the liquid reduced to half. This will take about ¾ hour.

CHICKEN/DUCKLING CURRY

* 2 units butter
* 4 units onions, finely chopped
* 1 unit curry powder
* 1 small chicken or young duckling (or 2 pigeons)
* Salt and pepper to taste
* Water

Divide the chicken into neat joints. Heat the butter and add the curry powder and onions. Fry until brown. Add the chicken and fry until brown. Add salt and 1 pint of hot water. Stir and simmer till tender. There should be about ½ pint of gravy. Potatoes may be added at the same time as the hot water. Coriander seed can be added but does not suit all tastes. Take a small spoonful of coriander and roast in a pan for a few moments. Bruise it to remove husks, pound finely in a mortar and add to the curry powder.

CHICKEN CURRY WITH FRUIT

* Leftover cold chicken picked from the carcase
* 1 apple
* 1 medium onion
* 1 tablespoon curry powder
* 1 clove of garlic
* ½ a green pepper
* ½ pint of chicken stock
* ½ cup sultanas
* 1 oz butter
* A pinch of salt and pepper

Put the chicken bones into a pan and cover with water, bring to the boil and simmer for 15 minutes. Strain and keep to one side. Peel and slice the onion. Remove the seeds from the pepper and cut into small pieces. Peel and chop the garlic. Heat the butter in a pan and add the onion. Fry until nearly soft and beginning to take on colour, then add the curry powder and stir for a minute. Remove the core and pips from the apple (but keep the skin), and chop roughly. Add the green pepper, chicken pieces, sultanas and apple to the curry. Pour on the chicken stock, season with salt and pepper and bring to the boil. Reduce the heat and simmer quietly while cooking the rice. Serve hot with a green vegetable.

COUNTRY CAPTAIN

- 1 small chicken
- ¼ lb ghee
- ½ lb onions, sliced
- 1 teaspoonful salt
- ½ teaspoonful powdered chillies
- ½ teaspoonful turmeric
- Water

Cut the chicken into pieces. Heat the ghee and fry the onions until crisp and brown and set aside. Fry the turmeric and chillies in the same pan for 2 minutes, stirring, then add the chicken with the salt. Continue stirring over the fire until the chicken is tender. Cover the curry with the fried onions after dishing and serve very hot with rice.

If using a larger chicken, add ¼ pint of hot water and let the curry simmer until this has been absorbed.

Cold chicken or lamb (cut into small pieces) can be cooked in this dish as against fresh meat. Melt 2 oz of ghee in a pan and add the meat mixed with some chillies cut up, a teaspoonful of salt, a large quantity of sliced onions and fry until the onions are quite tender.

STUFFED TRIPE

Make a stuffing of breadcrumbs, sage and seasoning mixed with a little milk. Take a large piece of tripe, spread the mixture thickly on half of it. Fold over the other half and sew edges together. Put in a greased baking tin, cover with two slices of bacon and cook for 1 hour. Serve with bacon gravy and mashed potatoes.

BRAINS SOUFFLE

Soak brains for a short time in salt and water, then boil up (take out strings). Beat up in a basin with 2 tablespoons of flour, 2 eggs, ½ cup of milk, a squeeze of lemon and a sprinkle of nutmeg, pepper and salt. Pour into a greased pie dish and bake for ½ hour in a good oven.

Vegetable and Savoury Dishes

Burtas are macedoines of vegetables and are useful for using up the remains. They are constantly served at breakfast. Potato burta is mashed potato mixed with fried onions and well seasoned. An excellent variation is cabbage and potato. Bringal burta (aubergine) is a great favourite. The bringals are roasted in the ashes and the skins removed. The pulp is then mashed and fried with a little butter and seasoning, including lime juice.

PLAIN BOILED RICE

This provides the supporting act to the main course.

For 2 people take 1 cup of rice. Put in a pan and cover with cold water. Wash the rice well, squeezing and rubbing the raw grains with your hand – the water will become cloudy. Drain, wash again and repeat the process a third time.

When ready to cook, add a pint of water and ¼ teaspoonful of salt to the rice. Cover the pan and bring to the boil. Do not stir. Reduce the heat and simmer quietly for about 15 minutes until tender.

Remove from the heat and strain through a sieve. Immediately rinse quickly with cold water. Steam the rice in the sieve over the pan. This will dry the rice.

CHITCHKEE CURRY

Slice some fresh onions. Fry them in plenty of butter. Mix some curry powder to a little paste with a little gravy. Add to the butter, fry slightly, then put in an olla podrida [olla podrida is a Spanish stew, made from chickpeas, beans and other vegetables with an assortment of meat – whatever is at hand] of boiled or fried vegetables. The greater the variety the better, and simmer till the whole is done. Serve with rice.

KITCHEREE 1

Into 4 units of boiling ghee fry 4 units of sliced onions, cut lengthways. Remove. Add 4 units of well-washed rice and 4 units of dhal. Fry until the butter is absorbed. Add some slices of green ginger, peppercorns, salt, cloves and cardamoms to taste and a stick or two of cinnamon. Just cover with water and simmer in a covered pan till almost quite dry. Care is required not to let the contents brown. They should be shaken up occasionally and stirred with a wooden spoon. Serve with fried onions scattered over the top.

KITCHEREE 2

- ½ pint lentils
- ½ pint rice
- 1 large onion
- 3 beads [cloves] garlic
- 24 cloves
- 3 bay leaves
- 2 sticks cinnamon
- 2 blades mace
- 12 cardamoms (seeds only)
- 3 quarts water

Wash lentils and place in boiling water with all the spices, the onion, etc. Let them boil for 5 minutes till the lentils change colour but are not soft. Then add the rice. Stir and watch carefully. As soon as the rice is cooked, strain through a colander and set to steam for about ½ hour. Remove onion and all spices and garnish with hard-boiled egg and fried onion.

VEGETABLE SAUG

* 2 lb spinach
* ½ teaspoon salt
* 1 oz ghee
* 4 oz sliced onions
* 1 whole fresh chilli or ½ teaspoon powdered chillies

Heat the ghee and fry half the onions to a good brown colour. Put in the washed spinach, the chilli (whole) and the remainder of the onions. No water. Stir, put on lid, and simmer for 10 minutes. Remove the lid and stir over the fire for 3 or 4 minutes till the spinach is soft and of a dark colour. Stir in the salt, drain off the water and serve very hot in a dish by itself to be eaten with curry, dhal and rice.

POTATO PIE

* 1 lb potatoes
* 1-2 oz butter
* ¼ pint milk
* Salt and pepper
* Ready-cooked brown meat stew of chicken, mutton or beef (can be leftover from a previous meal)

Peel the potatoes and cut in half or quarters and cook in salted water. Drain, and mash them, mixing in milk and butter to taste (a rich mash is required). Spoon a layer of potato on the bottom of a pie dish and cover with the nicely browned stew. Cover with remaining potato and bake for 15 minutes till brown.

POTATO BURTA

* ½ lb boiled potatoes
* ½ teaspoonful salt
* 1 teaspoonful onions
* 1 green chilli or ½ teaspoonful dried chillies

Let the potatoes cool and mash them with salt till smooth, then add the chopped onions and chillies. The addition of pure Indian mustard oil is an improvement. When well mixed, heap the potato on to a small plate and shape it like a bun. Mark into quarters with a knife but do not cut through to the bottom. Serve cold as a relish with curry, dhal or rice or cold meat.

BRINGAL BURTA

Bake a good-sized bringal in the oven (or in the ashes) till soft. Scoop out the flesh and mash with a little salt, a green chilli sliced or a little cayenne and a very little chopped raw onion. Serve cold as a relish with curry or rice, or cold meat.

STEWED DHAL

Fry 4 onions in 1 unit of butter or fat till brown. Add also 1 unit of curry powder, then 5 units of washed lentils to 5 units of thin stock. Stew till tender, adding more stock if required. It should be of the consistency of porridge. Serve with boiled rice or rice kedgeree.

DHAL POOREE

5 units of dhal, washed. Boil till tender. Add 1 unit of ground onions, ¼ unit of ground chillies, ¼ unit of ginger and turmeric mixed, a clove of garlic and ¼ teaspoon salt. Mix well.

Brown 6 onions in 2 units of butter and stir in the dhal. Make a flour and water paste as for water biscuits (recipe page 195). Take a piece of this the size of a walnut and hollow into a saucer. Put into this a sufficient quantity of the prepared dhal. Lay on another similar saucer of the paste, flute the edges and roll out as thinly as possible. When the size of a dinner plate fry in boiling ghee.

DHAL CHURCHURREE

* ½ lb dhal (red lentils)
* 1½ oz sliced onions
* 1 oz ghee
* 1 teaspoonful turmeric
* Pinch of salt
* 1 teaspoonful powdered chillies or 1 green chilli, sliced
* 2 bay leaves

Heat the ghee in a saucepan and fry the onions till brown and crisp, put them to one side and fry the dhal. When the ghee is absorbed, add the turmeric, salt, chillies and bay leaves with sufficient hot water to cover the dhal. Cover the pan and let it boil quietly, add more hot water if necessary, till the dhal is quite tender.

Take the pan off the heat and let it rest with the cover on to dry. Remove the bay leaves before serving and garnish with the fried onions. A green apple, pared and cut in quarters, may be added when the dhal is half cooked.

RICE AND DHAL

Cook rice with dhal. Serve with poached eggs and curry sauce. Delicious.

EGG CURRY

* 6 eggs
* 2 oz ghee
* 2 oz chopped onions
* 1 tablespoon curry powder
* ¼ teaspoonful salt
* 1 salt spoon ground pepper
* Water

Boil the eggs till hard, and dip in cold water and shell. Prick all over with a fork* and rub with a little curry powder and salt. Heat the ghee and put in the eggs whole and fry for 5 minutes, shaking the pan so they do not burn. Remove the eggs and fry half the onions. Add the curry powder and fry it well, stirring all the time. Add ¼ pint of hot water, let it boil a few minutes but do not stir. Return the eggs to the pan, a ¼ pint more water and the rest of the onions. Cover and simmer for ½ hour. Add the pepper before serving. There should be a rich, thick gravy.

* If using a silver fork, to remove staining formed by the eggs, put the fork into an aluminium pan with a teaspoonful of salt and a little boiling water. The stain will disappear.

DHAL AND EGG CURRY

* 5 eggs
* ½ lb dhal or split peas
* 2 oz butter
* 2 oz onions
* 1 unit curry powder
* ½ teaspoonful salt
* 1 salt spoonful ground pepper
* ¾ pint boiling water

If using split peas, soak for 12 hours in cold water. If using dhal wash thoroughly and soak in water for ½ hour. Boil the eggs till hard, and dip in cold water and shell. Prick all over with a fork and rub with a little curry powder and salt. Set aside.

Heat the butter and put in the eggs whole and fry for 5 minutes, shaking the pan so they do not burn. Remove the eggs and fry half the onions to a nice brown and add the curry powder and fry it well with the onions.

When the powder is well fried, it should be a rich brown not black.

Put in the split peas or dhal, stir well and let it cook for 5 minutes. Add ¼ pint of hot water. As soon as this is absorbed, add the whole eggs, the salt, the remainder of the onions, with ½ pint more hot water. Cover the saucepan and simmer till all the water absorbed and the dhal fully swelled and tender. Make sure it does not burn on the bottom of the pan. Add the pepper and serve very hot.

BACON AND EGG PIE

Line a small tin with pastry. Chop finely 3 bacon rashers. Strew it over the pastry and over it break 4 eggs. Put a teaspoon of butter on each egg, sprinkle with salt and pepper and a grating of nutmeg. Cover with a crust and glaze. Bake slowly for ½ hour.

POACHED EGGS IN MILK

Half fill a poaching pan with milk. Drop in required number of eggs. Thicken the milk. Add chopped parsley and pour the sauce over the eggs.

PARIS TOAST

Boil 4 eggs hard and quarter. Chop an onion fine and fry in butter. Add 1 teaspoon of flour, beat till smooth. Add 1 cup of milk. Stir till it thickens. Put in pepper and salt. Heat the eggs in this mixture and pour on to hot buttered toast.

FRIED WHOLE EGGS

Instead of whole hard-boiled eggs, lightly poach the eggs until set, carefully remove from the pan with a slotted spoon and then roll in fresh breadcrumbs before frying in ghee.

Boil the eggs lightly and carefully remove the shell. Roll in fresh breadcrumbs. Heat some butter and/or oil in a pan and fry till golden brown.

POACHED EGGS WITH TOMATOES

* 6 large ripe tomatoes
* 4 eggs
* 1 oz butter
* ½ teaspoonful salt
* A little pepper
* A small piece of onion for flavour

Pierce the skins of the tomatoes with the point of a knife and put into a bowl. Cover with boiling water and leave for a minute, then drain and peel off the skin. Chop roughly.

Heat the butter in a deep frying pan and fry the piece of onion in it till quite brown, then discard. Pour the mashed tomatoes on to the boiling butter and keep stirring over the fire till it is of a rich, dark colour. Add the salt. Stop stirring and break the eggs on to the tomatoes taking care not to break the yolks. As soon as the eggs set firm, lift them out with a slice and arrange neatly in a dish. Dust with the pepper and pour the tomatoes around them. Serve at once very hot. A nice breakfast dish.

EGG FRITTERS

Sprinkle some slices of hard-boiled egg with chopped parsley, salt and pepper and dip into batter and fry.

RUMBLED EGGS

* 3 eggs
* ¼ pint milk
* ¼ oz butter
* ¼ teaspoonful salt
* A very little powdered chilli or ½ a small fresh chilli, finely shredded

Beat the eggs with the salt and the chilli. Add the milk and the butter, broken up into small pieces. Put the eggs into a small basin and set it in a saucepan of boiling water over the fire. Keep stirring till the eggs set, but do not let them harden. It should be more like a very thick custard than a firm scrambled egg dish. Serve on toast or in a small dish.

DEVILLED EGGS

* 4 eggs
* ½ oz butter
* ¼ pint of stock
* A little pepper
* ½ teaspoonful salt
* ½ teaspoonful cayenne
* 1 teaspoonful mustard
* 1 tablespoon Worcestershire sauce
* 1 teaspoonful finely chopped onions

Boil the eggs till hard, dip into cold water and remove the shells. Cut each through the middle into two halves. Slip out the yolks and cut a tiny piece off the pointed end of each half white, so that the pieces may stand up like cups. Mash the yolks into a paste with half the butter, a very little salt, a little pepper and the ½ teaspoonful of cayenne. Fill the paste back into the whites of the eggs and arrange them neatly in a dish.

Fry the onions in the remainder of the butter, and as soon as they brown put in the salt, mustard and sauce, which should be mixed together before adding to the onions. Stir all these together over the fire for 3–4 minutes. Then add the stock thoroughly heated, stir together, pour over the eggs and serve at once.

OMELETTE INDIAN STYLE

* 6 eggs
* 1 oz butter
* ½ teaspoonful salt
* ½ teaspoonful shredded onions
* ½ teaspoonful powdered chillies or 1 fresh chilli
* 1 teaspoonful chopped parsley

Separate the yolks and whites of the eggs. Beat the yolks in a basin with the salt, chillies, onions and the parsley till very light. Beat the whites to a firm snow.

Heat the butter in a medium-sized pan and when boiling, beat the whites of the eggs lightly with the yolks and pour into the frying pan at once. Do not stir. As soon as the omelette sets, fold it over with a slice and when lightly browned, slip it on to a hot dish and serve at once.

CHEESE RAMEKINS

* 1 oz butter
* ½ oz flour
* ¼ gill milk
* 2 eggs
* 2 oz grated cheese
* Pepper and salt

Put each egg into a buttered ramekin. Mix the flour with the milk. Add the salt and pepper and pour over the egg. Dot with the butter and grated cheese. Bake in a bain marie for about 10 minutes. The whites should be firm, the yolks soft and runny.

EGG BURTA

Boil 1 or more eggs until hard. Peel and chop finely but do not mash. Mix with salt, pepper, a small quantity of finely shredded raw onion and green chilli. Serve heaped on a plate with rice or curry.

STEWED PEAS

Put 24 units of peas into a stew pan with 1 unit of butter. Fill up with water and then, with the hands, rub the butter into the peas. Pour off the water, add a large lettuce, shredded finely, 2 whole green onions and 1 unit of parsley, salt and ½ unit of sugar. Stew with the lid on for ½ hour. Reduce if there is much liquid, remove the parsley and onions and add a little light glaze of flour and thicken. (The lettuce may be omitted.)

PEAS A LA PARISIENNE

As left, only with the addition of 2 cloves and a little winter savory. The cooking must be done in a tightly closed vessel over a marked fire and the pan must be shaken occasionally.

FRENCH BEANS A LA PROVENCALE

* 1 unit boiled and chopped onions
* 1 unit olive oil
* Some chopped parsley
* Salt and pepper
* 1 unit tarragon vinegar
* Boiled French beans

Fry onions, parsley, salt and pepper in the oil, add the beans and lastly the vinegar.

TOMATOES AND PARSLEY

Slice any number of tomatoes in a fireproof china dish. Put in layers with plenty of minced parsley. Season with pepper and salt. Cover with browned breadcrumbs. Baste with butter. Bake in a hot oven and serve.

STUFFED TOMATOES

Slice off stalk end of large, ripe tomatoes and scoop out the seeds and pulp with a spoon taking care not to scoop too much. To every tablespoon of pulp add 1 tablespoon of fresh breadcrumbs, ½ tablespoon of chopped, hard-boiled eggs, whipped cream, a suspicion of onion, salt and pepper. Mix to a rather liquid farce. Fry 3 tablespoons of fresh breadcrumbs in a little ghee. Fill the tomatoes with the stuffing and cover with the fried breadcrumbs and a grate of cheese.

Bake till bubbling and brown (15–20 minutes) and serve with the remainder of the pulp made into a thin purée made with ordinary stock.

TOMATOES A LA PROVENCALE 1

Proceed as above but make the farce with 2 tablespoons of bacon or ham, ½ tablespoon of chopped parsley and onion, 2 tablespoons of mushrooms and 1 or 2 egg yolks. Fill the tomatoes with 2 tablespoons of salad oil. Place in a pre-heated oven.

TOMATOES A LA PROVENCALE 2

As above but make the farce with 2 units of chopped onion and parsley, 2 units of chopped mushrooms and 2 yolks of egg. Fill the tomatoes and stew in a pan with 2 units of salad oil for 15–20 minutes.

TOMATOES A LA PROVENCALE 3

Slice off the top of each tomato, take out the pips and scoop out the inside. Have ready a stuffing of breadcrumbs, parsley, onions, tarragon, salt, pepper and oil. Mix this with the tomato pulp and replace in the rinds. Let them cook in the oven for 40 minutes. If the tomatoes are watery, drain off before you mix the stuffing.

TOMATO CUSTARDS

Proceed as for stuffed tomatoes [recipe page 126] but use the pulp removed to make a good thick tomato purée, adding of course flavouring of chopped onion or garlic and red pepper. To every 2 tablespoons add 1 yolk of egg. Fill the tomatoes with the mixture, grate a little cheese over the top and bake on a buttered tin for 15–20 minutes. A little cream may be added if procurable.

TOMATO SOUFFLE

One slice of bread soaked in 3 units of milk or water to a paste. 5 units raw pulp of ripe tomatoes, ½ unit butter, 1 unit grated cheese, onion juice, cayenne and salt to taste. Then add 2 egg yolks and fold in 3 egg whites well whisked and sprinkle grated cheese over. Bake in a buttered soufflé dish until well risen and golden brown, approximately 30–35 minutes. Enough for 3 people.

TOMATO SANDWICHES

Pulp 3 large tomatoes. Reduce by boiling. Add ½ unit of onion juice and salad oil, some salt, pepper, cayenne and sugar. Pound 4 hard-boiled yolks of egg with 2 units of butter and ½ unit of Harvey's sauce (recipe page 36). Make into sandwiches.

FRIED MARROW AND TOMATO

Cut some young vegetable marrows into rounds. Flour them well and fry them in butter. Then put them in a stew pan with some good stock, flavoured with tomato juice, and let them simmer gently till tender. Serve with the gravy they are cooked in.

BEETROOT AS A FULL MEAL

Boil beetroot (1 large not damaged). Take skin off and grate it and put in a saucepan with a lump of butter and a teaspoon of vinegar and some allspice (½ teaspoon). Let it simmer for 5 or 10 minutes, then mash into it the same quantity of potatoes (want about 2 lb potatoes to 1 large beetroot). Brown some bacon – about 2 slices. Cut up and add with bacon fat.

Eat with sausages or anything. Nice to eat with a bit of brown gravy.

POMELO SALAD WITH LETTUCE

Pomelo with lettuce and a salad dressing composed of 3 parts of olive oil to 1 part of lemon juice – salt and pepper. Mix and pour over.

POTATO SCONES

16 units of mashed potato put into a basin and mixed with 1 unit of butter, 1 yolk of egg. Add some salt, 8 units of flour and, if necessary, a little milk. Roll out as thin as possible and cut into rounds. Toast or bake on a griddle. Butter, pile one on top of the other. Divide into two with a sharp knife and serve as muffins.

BAKED POTATO PUFF

Rub through a sieve sufficient cold potatoes to fill a small basin. Add 2 tablespoons of melted butter and beat until the potatoes look white and smooth. Beat 1 egg to which is added 4 tablespoons of milk. Mix with the potatoes, season to taste and put in a buttered dish and bake until a golden brown and puffed up.

POTATOES MAITRE D'HOTEL

1 lb boiled potatoes. Slice and warm in a pan with 2 oz melted butter and chopped parsley. Put into a dish and pour over ¼ pint of white sauce. Add a squeeze of lemon and serve very hot.

SPAGHETTI D'ESPAGNE

* ½ tin mulligatawny soup
* 3 tomatoes
* 3 onions
* 3 pieces of cheese the size of a walnut
* ¼ lb spaghetti

Put the soup, chopped tomatoes and onions in a saucepan and cook gently for 20 minutes. Then add cheese and cook for another 20 minutes. When ready, strain through a colander. Take ¼ lb best spaghetti and boil until cooked in boiling salted water. When cooked, drain and pour over sauce. Let it stand to keep hot for ¼ hour and serve with grated cheese handed separately. Use as a separate course or with chicken or steak.

BATTER

* 4 oz sifted flour
* Little salt
* Little pepper

Mix gradually to a stiff paste with 2 egg yolks, 2 tablespoons of salad oil. Whip the whites of 2 eggs to a stiff froth and beat them in lightly 10 minutes before use. The rest should be made several hours before use. Or use the white of 1 egg and add 1 gill of tepid water to the batter custard.

BLANQUETTE OF TURNIPS

Boil 1 lb of white turnips. When cold slice and lay in a pie dish with thick scalded cream between each layer. Season with pepper and salt and heat through. Any cooking is disastrous.

ENDIVE OR LETTUCE WITH CREAM

Wash in several waters. Plunge in boiling salt and water and when quite tender drain in a colander, carefully squeezing out the moisture. Chop and pass through a coarse wire sieve.

Put in a stew pan with 1 unit of butter, a little nutmeg and salt. After 10 minutes' slow boiling and add ¼ unit of sugar, 3 units of cream and 1 unit of thick white sauce. Reduce to a thick purée and serve, like spinach, with croutons.

CUCUMBERS WITH WHITE SAUCE

Cut the cucumbers about an inch thick, steep for several hours in salt and vinegar. Pour away the moisture and stew for ½ hour in 2 units of butter, ½ unit of sugar and a little nutmeg. Pour off the juice, add a little white sauce, 3 units of cream in which 2 yolks of egg have been mixed, ½ unit of lemon juice and chopped parsley.

CUCUMBER MAITRE D'HOTEL

Slice as for salad and fry in butter with chopped parsley, green onions and a pinch of herbs.

BUBBLE AND SQUEAK

Place small, thin slices of cold salt beef in a frying pan, taking care to have plenty of fat bits. Fry, without drying. Set the meat aside and in the same pan put sufficient previously boiled and chopped cabbage. Fry sharply. Add the meat but save a few pieces for garnishing. Let the whole bubble and squeak well in the pan. Serve very hot in a pyramid and garnished with the pieces of meat which were set aside.

VEGETABLE CURRY

Vegetable curries may be varied indefinitely.

- 1 lb potatoes
- 1 lb peas
- 1 small cauliflower
- 1 tablespoon curry powder
- 2 oz ghee
- 2 oz onions, chopped
- 1 teaspoonful salt
- ½ pint water

Peel and cut the potatoes into quarters and the cauliflower into neat pieces. Heat the ghee and fry half the quantity of onions till brown, stir in the curry powder, frying it well with the onions. In a couple of minutes add the water and salt. Bring to the boil, then add the vegetables with the remainder of the onions. Cover the pan and simmer for an hour. There should be little or no gravy.

PUFTALOONS WITH BACON

Mix 1½ cups of flour with enough milk to make a firm dough (about a small cup of liquid). Roll out on to a floured surface to ¼ inch thick and cut into rounds. Fry in hot fat until golden brown, turning once. While these are cooking fry some bacon in another pan and serve together with grilled tomatoes.

ASPARAGUS WITH CREAM

This makes a very sophisticated first course or light lunch.

- 2-3 oz butter
- Yolk of one egg
- Green onions
- Chopped parsley
- Juice of half a lemon
- Cream
- A little sugar
- Salt and pepper
- Large bunch of asparagus

Make rather a thick sauce of melted butter with a seasoning of chopped green onions and parsley. Add cream and yolk of one egg, a little sugar, the juice of half a lemon, salt and pepper. Cut up the cooked asparagus into pieces, put in the sauce and serve on croutons [recipe page 134].

GNOCCHI

- ¼ cup butter
- ¼ cup flour
- ¼ cup cornflour
- ½ teaspoonful salt
- 2 cups hot milk
- ¾ cup grated cheese
- 2 egg yolks

Melt the butter and add the flours. Blend well and add the hot milk and beaten egg yolks. Then add ½ cup of cheese and the salt. Cook together for a few minutes. Pour into a buttered dish to cool. When firm enough to cut into small pieces, arrange in a buttered dish, sprinkle with the remaining cheese and brown well in a hot oven.

CROUSTADES – CROUTONS

Stale loaf, close grained, cut into slices 2 inch thick, then rounds and small rounds for lid. If the croutons to be soaked and fried leave at least ¼ inch thick wall. Drain for a minute or two and then fry at once.

With sweet custard flavoured with essences makes a delicate and pretty pudding. Very good with custard made with a little broth and yolk of egg. When cold, brush with white of egg and sprinkle with chopped parsley or lobster or bacon.

BAKED CHEESE

Take some very thin slices of toast. Spread with thick cream. Dust with a layer of grated cheese. Make these into sandwiches and cut in strips, put in a dish in the bottom of which equal parts of grated cheese, thin cream and beer or white wine have been mixed. Put in the oven until the cheese has melted.

CHEESE TOAST

* 2 oz cheese
* 1 egg
* Cayenne
* ½ gill milk
* Buttered toast
* Salt

ORANGE SALAD FOR WILD DUCK

Remove all skins and pith from the oranges, cut into natural divisions and season with salad oil, a little brandy, a teaspoon of caster sugar and a teaspoon of finely chopped chervil or tarragon.

Puddings

ZANDRINA PUDDING

A most delicious pudding but the ingredients must be well and separately mixed.

* Weight of 3 eggs the same size of:
* Butter with the salt rubbed out
* The same of finely powdered sugar
* Same of flour
* Raspberry jam

Beat the butter to a cream then add the sugar, yolks of eggs and a large tablespoon of raspberry jam. Mix with the same quantity of cold water – then add the flour. Stir all well together and lastly pour in gently the whites of eggs beaten to a stiff froth. Put the mixture into a mould and boil for 3 hours. Serve with jam and arrowroot sauce.

MUNDAH

Equal quantities of desiccated coconut and sugar. Mix well with condensed milk. Place in a greased dish and bake till golden brown.

PRINCESS ROYAL CUSTARD

* 8 fresh eggs, separated
* 1 dessertspoon cornflour
* Sugar to taste
* 4 units almonds, blanched, peeled and bruised in a mortar
* 2 pints milk

Beat the egg yolks in a deep bowl. Add the cornflour, beating well. Add enough sugar to taste. Add the bruised almonds and pour the mixture into a saucepan. Stir in the milk and put the pan on a brisk flame. Stir continuously and once it has come to the boil reduce the flame and stir for a further 15 minutes until thickened.

Fill the custard cups or glasses within ½ inch of the top. A quarter of an hour before service, whisk the egg whites, flavouring with essence of almonds or orange flower water during the process. Spoon on to the custard and serve.

ORANGE CUSTARD

* 1 orange
* 1 unit brandy
* 4 units sugar
* 4 egg yolks
* 1 pint milk

Pare the rind from half the orange and boil in water until very tender. Remove and pound to a fine pulp. Add the brandy, juice of the orange, sugar and egg yolks, mixing well. Beat for 10 minutes. Bring the milk to the boil and slowly add to the egg mixture. Beat until cold. Pour into custard cups, stand in a dish of hot water and bake until set. This may be served hot or cold.

SWEET BAKED BATTER PUDDING

* 2 eggs
* 2½ tablespoons flour
* Pinch of salt
* About ½ pint milk

Mix and beat well as for ordinary batter and pour into a pie dish that has not only been well buttered but has had a dot or two of butter on the bottom. Bake for 15 minutes. Remove from the oven and drop 4 tablespoons of any kind of jam on the surface. Put back into the oven and continue baking for a further 15–20 minutes until risen and golden brown. (The jam falls to the bottom.) Very good.

BAKED RAISIN PUDDING

* ½ lb flour
* 6 oz stoned Valencia raisins
* 2 oz shredded suet
* ½ oz caster sugar
* Pinch of salt
* Milk to make the consistency of thick batter
* Grated nutmeg if liked

Mix all together and bake for ¾ hour–1 hour in buttered pie dish. Turn out and serve with sugar. This recipe can be improved with the addition of candied peel, currants and an egg.

MARGARET PUDDING

Rub 2 oz of butter into 4 oz of flour, add 2 oz of sugar and a teaspoon of baking powder, 1 teacup of milk and one egg. Butter a basin, put a layer of jam at the bottom and pour the mixture over the jam. Steam for 1 hour.

AUNT LOUISA

* ½ pint grated breadcrumbs
* 1 pint milk
* 3 oz caster sugar
* 1 oz butter
* ½ lemon peel and juice
* 3 eggs (Indian eggs being smaller, perhaps try 2)

Pour over the breadcrumbs ¾ pint of milk (warm). Stir it well together and add the remainder of the milk with the grated lemon peel, half the sugar, the butter and the yolks of the eggs, well beaten.

Mix all thoroughly together and pour into an oven dish and bake carefully.

Put the juice of the lemon into a basin, add the remainder of the sugar, beat it well and add the whites of the eggs well whisked to a very stiff froth.

Put a layer of jam on the top of the pudding, pile the whisked whites of the eggs on top, place in an oven and bake lightly.

WATER ICES

* 20 units water
* 24 units sugar
* Add 20 units of any fruit juice

Of course, where fruit is very strong, as in lemon juice, it must be diluted in water. Some fruits, as melon, peaches, apricots, pineapple, are best pulped and pushed through a sieve. Mango ice is also good made this way and an addition of mint if liked will improve flavour.

CREME SUPREME (SOPHIE GRISBACH'S RECIPE)

* A little clear jelly to decorate the mould with
* ¾ pint cream
* 6 leaves gelatine, or ½ pint aspic/Nelson's gelatine
* ½ teacup cold water
* ¼ lb glacé fruits
* 1 lemon
* 3 oz loaf sugar
* 3 tablespoons sherry
* 1 tablespoon brandy

Cut the fruits into little pieces. Rub sugar on to the rind of the lemon, pound it and dissolve the gelatine in water. Add it to the sugar. With lemon juice, sherry and brandy whisk the cream till quite still (be careful not to overwhisk it). Add the gelatine when cool but not setting, and fruits. Turn into the mould and when quite set, dip into warm water right up to the top and turn out. Let the cream set a little before turning into the mould. Don't turn the fruits into the cream altogether but drop them only one by one while the cream is setting.

CUSTARD (MOTHER'S [FRANCES CHARLOTTE CAMPBELL])

* 4 eggs (yolks only)
* 1 tumbler milk (½ pint)
* 1½ tablespoons white sugar
* Vanilla essence

Well beat the yolks, add the milk and sugar 'warmed' on to the yolks. Cook in a jug slowly sufficiently thickened. When cold add essence.

CREAMED ICES FOR PRESERVED FRUIT

* 1 pint milk
* 1 gill cream
* 3 yolks eggs
* Sugar to taste
* 6 oz preserved fruit pulp or jam, such as strawberry, raspberry, greengage, apricot, peach or pineapple

Beat the egg yolks, add the milk and the cream. When nearly boiling, replace in the stewpan and stir by the side of the fire until it thickens – but the mixture must not boil. Strain. Add the sieved fruit or jam.

FRUIT CREAMS

Fruit creams are made with the pulp of ripe fruit in the proportion of half pulp and half whipped cream or with jam rubbed through a sieve after being moistened with water, or with syrup.

To make strawberry or raspberry cream from jam take 2 units of chip or powdered gelatine and dissolve in 5 units of water. Whisk 10 units of cream, add 5 units of syrup or pulped jam and the dissolved gelatine. Colour with cochineal.

Peach or apricot or any other fruit cream can be made by pulping the fresh fruit with sugar to taste and adding to every 10 units of pulp, 10 units of whipped cream and a little more than the above proportion of gelatine dissolved in 5 units of water.

CHOCOLATE PUDDING

* 2 oz butter
* 3 oz sugar
* 2 eggs
* ½ cup milk
* Few drops of vanilla extract
* 6 oz self-raising flour
* Pinch of salt
* 1 tablespoon cocoa

Cream the butter and sugar together until light and fluffy. Beat in the eggs, one by one. Add the milk and vanilla extract and beat well. Sieve the flour and cocoa together to remove any lumps and fold into the batter. Mix in the pinch of salt and pour into a well-greased pudding basin. Cover with greaseproof paper and steam for 1½–2 hours. Serve with a sweet sauce such as custard or chocolate flavoured sauce.

BLACK CAP PUDDING

* 1 large cup self-raising flour
* 1 small cup sugar
* 2 oz butter
* 1 egg
* ½ cup milk
* Dark jam such as blackberry or blackcurrant

Butter a pudding basin and put 2–3 tablespoons of jam in the bottom. Rub the flour, butter and sugar together. Beat the egg with the milk and add to the dry ingredients to make a smooth batter. Pour into the basin on top of the jam, cover with greaseproof paper and steam for 2 hours. Make a sauce by diluting a little extra jam with some boiling water and serve separately.

BAKED RICE

* ½ cup short rice
* 2 tablespoons sugar
* 1 pint milk
* Few drops essence of lemon
* Few knobs butter
* Shavings of fresh nutmeg

Wash the rice and lay in the bottom of a buttered pie dish. Sprinkle on the sugar and add the milk, lemon essence and butter. Grate over fresh nutmeg. Bake slowly for 1 hour. If the milk is absorbed, add a little more by prodding any skin which has formed so that the milk mixes well with the rice. It must be creamy.

TAPIOCA JELLY

* 1½ oz tapioca
* 1½ pints water
* Lemon juice
* Sugar
* Port

Wash the tapioca and soak in water for 4 hours. Simmer in the same water, adding a little more if necessary. When the tapioca is clear, it is cooked. Add flavouring and pour into mould or glasses to cool and set.

SAGO JELLY

5 units of sago well washed. Boil to a jelly in 25 units of water. Add 5 units of raspberry vinegar and 1 unit of redcurrant jelly. Colour with cochineal and pour into a mould. Or: use 20 units of water and 3 each of sugar, lime juice and sherry. Tapioca can be used the same way – about 3 units are sufficient. Arrowroot or cornflour also make good jellies. The proportions will be rather more than 1 unit to 20 of liquid.

BAKED PUDDING

* 3 units caster sugar
* 3 units butter
* 3 eggs, separated
* ½ lb strawberry jam
* 2 units breadcrumbs
* 1 lemon plus 1 unit juice from 2nd lemon
* Puff pastry

Line a baking dish with the pastry and spread with the jam. Cream the butter and sugar until pale in colour. Add the egg yolks, one by one, working in well. Add the breadcrumbs and lemon rind and juice. Mix well and pour on top of the jam. Bake for 45 minutes. Stiffly beat the egg whites with a teaspoon of sugar and 1 unit of lemon juice. Pour this over the pudding ¾ of the way through cooking.

SHORT CRUST FOR SWEET TARTS

* 1 lb flour
* ½ lb butter
* ¼ lb sugar
* 2 egg yolks
* 1 teacup of milk and water mixed

Mix all together to a paste and leave to rest for ½ hour before rolling out.

COCONUT MERINGUE FOR FILLING TARTLETS

* 1 oz fine breadcrumbs
* 1 oz desiccated coconut
* 2 oz caster sugar
* Pinch of salt
* 1 oz fresh butter
* Yolks of 2 eggs
* 1 pint milk (try ½ or ¼)

Put the milk into a saucepan. When it nearly boils, add to it the sugar, salt, crumbs, coconut and butter and let it all boil together for a brief moment and then pour on to the beaten egg yolks. Now ready for use.

HALF-PAY PUDDING

An egg may be used, but then only half the quantity of milk. To make it more economical, add 1 cup of cold tea – this gives very good results.

* 1 cup flour
* 1 teaspoonful salt
* 1 teaspoonful bicarbonate of soda
* 1 cup fresh white breadcrumbs
* 1 cup dark (muscovado) sugar
* 1 cup of suet
* 1 cup mixed dried fruit: sultanas, raisins, currants
* Zest of ½ a lemon

Mix all the dry ingredients together. Blend the milk with the bicarbonate of soda and add to the other ingredients, mixing well. Pour into a buttered pudding basin and steam for 2½–3 hours. Serve with a sweet sauce.

APPLE CHARLOTTE

Butter a pie dish and cover the bottom with fresh white breadcrumbs. Stew approximately 2 lb of apples with some sugar to taste and spoon over the breadcrumbs. Cover with a thick layer of raisins and another thick layer of breadcrumbs. Dot with butter and bake until brown for about 30 minutes.

COCONUT PUDDING

* 2 units desiccated coconut
* 3 units caster sugar
* 2 eggs
* ½ pint milk

Beat the sugar with the egg yolks till light and fluffy. Add the milk and coconut, mixing well. Stir in the stiffly beaten egg whites. Pour into a buttered dish and bake for 20 minutes in a brisk oven.

COFFEE JUNKET

1 pint of fresh milk (reserve 1 gill). Bring to the boil and pour over a tablespoon of coarsely ground coffee. Allow this to infuse for 10–15 minutes. Strain, sweeten and add remainder of the milk. Warm gently to blood heat. Remove from the fire and add 1 teaspoonful of prepared rennet. Pour custard into glasses. Whip and sweeten some cream and put on each glass.

COFFEE MOULD

* 1½ oz caster sugar
* ½ oz gelatine
* 1 pint milk
* 1 dessertspoon coffee essence

Boil the milk, then pour it on the gelatine. Stir in the sugar. Add the essence. Stir till cold and creamy before putting into a mould.

DUTCH BLANCMANGE (MOTHER'S [FRANCES CHARLOTTE CAMPBELL])

1 oz gelatine allowed to swell in a pint of water. Heat till dissolved. Add 6 oz of sugar, the yolks of 6 eggs beaten with 2 wineglasses of sherry and a glass of lemon juice. Heat all together but do not boil or eggs will curdle. Strain into a mould and leave to set. Half quantities sufficient for 4 people.

CLARET JELLY

Put 1 oz Nelson's gelatine to steep till it swells in a tumbler of water. Add 1 pint of claret, 4 cups of white sugar (7 oz is sufficient), a little lime juice, 1 tablespoon of brandy (or whisky), 1 tablespoon of port or liqueur. Dissolve the gelatine and sugar only and strain, then add wine.

UNCLE TOM

15 units of flour – mix into it ¼ unit of bicarbonate of soda and 10 units of chopped suet. Make into a stiff rocky paste with 2½ units of milk and 2½ units of golden syrup. Steam in a tightly covered mould for 2 hours. Leave plenty of room for it to rise.

By adding a little sugar, raisins, peel, an admirable children's pudding can be made.

BANANA JELLY

This is a delicious, light and tangy pudding.

* 3 ripe bananas
* ½ lb sugar
* 2 lemons
* 4-6 leaves gelatine
* ½ pint whipped cream
* Water

Peel the skin in strips from 1 lemon (without the pith) and then cut up the pulp of both lemons into very small pieces, again removing all the white pith, skin and pips. Put into a pan with the sugar and 1½ pints of water. Boil without a lid until the liquid is reduced to about a pint. Strain through a fine sieve and leave to get cold. Prepare the gelatine according to the instructions on the packet.

When the lemony juice is cold, stir in the prepared gelatine. Peel the bananas and slice thinly and add to the jelly. Leave to stand for 15 minutes until it begins to set – the banana slices will float to the top – and when the jelly is firmer, stir the fruit so that it is suspended in the juice. Wet the mould with cold water, drain and then carefully pour the jelly into it. Chill for at least 8 hours. When ready to serve, tip the jelly on to a plate and surround it with whipped cream.

BANANA PUFFS WITH MOCK CREAM

Use as many bananas as there are persons to be served. Roll in cinnamon and then in thin pie crust. Bake in a quick oven and serve with the following cream:

Beat a sliced banana with an egg white and continue beating till stiff. The banana forms a smooth paste with the egg white.

VANILLA CREAM

* Yolks of 3 eggs
* 1 pint milk
* Few drops vanilla essence
* ½ oz gelatine
* Sugar

Make a custard of the yolks of eggs and the milk. Sweeten and add the vanilla. Put back on the fire. Allow to heat until the custard has thickened. Dissolve the gelatine in ½ pint of boiling milk and stir into the custard. When cold, pour into a mould and let it stand till the next day.

CHOCOLATE CREAM

Mix 2 units of arrowroot smoothly with 3 units of cold water. Add 12 units of caster sugar and boil rapidly for 8–10 minutes, stirring continuously. Remove from the fire and stir till a little cool. Flavour with vanilla or rose essence and continue stirring till it creams, then roll into little balls.

Melt some chocolate over steam adding no water. When the cream balls are cold, roll them one by one in the melted chocolate and lay them on a buttered slab to cool. They can be varied by adding coconut, etc.

GOLDEN PUDDING

* 4 oz flour
* 2 oz breadcrumbs
* 2 oz light brown sugar
* 4 oz suet
* 2 tablespoons marmalade
* 1 egg
* ½ cup milk
* ½ teaspoonful bicarbonate of soda

Mix all the dry ingredients together and moisten with the egg (beaten) and marmalade. Add the milk and bicarbonate of soda and mix till smooth. Pour into a buttered basin and steam for 2½ hours. Serve with the following sauce:

* ½ pint boiling water
* 1 dessertspoon arrowroot
* Pinch of salt
* 2 tablespoons marmalade or golden syrup
* Butter

Mix the arrowroot in a pan with a little cold water to a smooth paste. Add the boiling water, stirring well and cook for a few minutes over a low fire. Stir in the marmalade or syrup, a pinch of salt and finish off the sauce with a small nut of butter, whisked in. Serve immediately.

DRIED FRUITS TO STEW

Pour fruit into an enamelled pan with sugar and flavouring and pour in enough boiling water to cover. Stir and replace the lid to keep in all the goodness. Do NOT put on the fire but let it stand for 12 hours. Then stew on the fire very gently till the fruit is quite soft. Remove from the fire but do not uncover till the fruit is cold. Excellent for prunes.

TO STEW A PUDDING IN A COMMON SAUCEPAN

When the mould is filled, tie it over just with a well-buttered paper and then with a small piece of muslin well floured. Gather up two corners and tie them carefully so that no part of the paper and muslin touch the water. Put a saucer upside down in the saucepan with enough water to cover to a depth of 3 inches and when it boils put in the mould, press on the cover of the saucepan and boil gently without ceasing till it is done. More boiling water must be added if it evaporates but it must be poured carefully without touching the pudding.

TREACLE PUDDING

- ½ lb flour
- ¼ lb suet (½ lb if shredded)
- 1 teaspoon ground ginger
- ½ teaspoon Yeatman's baking powder
- Teacup treacle (golden syrup)
- 1 gill milk
- 1 egg

To the flour add the chopped suet, baking powder and ginger. Beat up the egg in the milk and treacle and add them to the dry ingredients. Steam for 2 hours.

TOAST AND SYRUP PUDDING

- 4 thick slices bread
- 2 eggs
- ½ pint milk
- ½ lb sugar
- Butter
- 1 lemon
- Water

Remove the crusts from the bread. Beat the eggs and mix in the milk. Soak the bread in the milk and eggs for 15 minutes. Put some butter into a frying pan and when hot (not burning) carefully drop in the bread. Brown on both sides. Arrange on a warm dish. Make a syrup with the sugar and a sherry glass of water and boil till thick and add the juice of the lemon. Pour this over the toast when still boiling and serve immediately.

LEMON PUDDING

* 6 units sugar
* 4 units butter
* 6 eggs - the yolks and whites separated
* Juice of 2 lemons
* 4 units breadcrumbs

Cream the butter and sugar and add the yolks 2 at a time, mixing well. Add the lemon juice and the breadcrumbs. Lastly, add the well-beaten whites of the eggs. Pour into a buttered dish and bake for 20 minutes or until lightly browned. Serve immediately.

LEMON CHEESECAKE (MOTHER'S [FANNY CHARLOTTE BEGBIE])

* 4 chittacks butter
* 8 eggs
* 4 chittacks caster sugar
* Lemon juice to taste
* Lemon essence to taste

Melt 4 chittacks of butter in an enamelled saucepan, while mixing stir into it the well-beaten yolks of 8 eggs and the whites of 3 eggs and 4 chittacks of finely powdered white sugar (caster). When dissolved, add lemon juice according to taste and a few drops of lemon essence. Line a pudding dish with butter and bake or cook till thick. If the mixture oils add beaten-up yolk of another egg (without white).

Swift through the sparkling wave the vessel flies,
Her loftiest honors quivering in the skies.

1
2
3
4

Painted by R. Smirke, R.A. Engraved by Milton.

THE CONQUEST.

RICE CREAMS

* 20 units milk
* 10 units whipped cream
* 2 units white sugar
* 1 unit rice
* 1 unit arrowroot
* Vanilla or lemon essence

Boil the rice in 10 units of milk till quite soft and put aside. Boil the other 10 units of milk with the sugar and stir in the arrowroot. Boil till very stiff. Add the whipped cream and the flavouring and set in a mould. This is delicious iced and should be served up with apricot jam.

CHRISTMAS PUDDING 1

* 1 lb brown sugar
* 3 lb mixed fruit
* 1¼ lb breadcrumbs
* 12 oz Shreddo (suet)
* 1 cup flour
* 2 teaspoons mixed spice
* 1 teaspoon powdered nutmeg
* 12 eggs less 4 whites
* 1 teaspoon almond and lemon essence
* 2 glasses of sherry or some wine

Makes two puddings 4¼ lb each. Do puddings in cloths if short of bowls.

CHRISTMAS PUDDING 2

Put into a large pan 2 lb of large raisins, stoned but not chopped. Add: 1 lb sultanas, 2 lb currants, 2 lb breadcrumbs, 1 lb candied mixed peel (sliced), 2 lb good moist sugar (not too brown), 2 lb beef suet, 2 oz mixed spice, 1 teaspoon salt. Mix all thoroughly together and moisten with 16 eggs well beaten.

Stir in 1 gill of brandy, 1 teaspoonful of lemon essence, 1 teaspoonful of Ratafia essence [almond essence]. If not moist enough, add milk. Put in a large tablespoon of dried flour. Boil in a buttered and floured cloth (or pudding basins, greased) for 2–3 hours if wanted to keep before eating. Above is an Indian recipe and probably 8 or 12 eggs are sufficient.

XMAS PLUM PUDDING (MOTHER'S [FRANCES CHARLOTTE CAMPBELL])

* 2 lb large raisins
* 1 lb sultanas
* 2 lb currants
* 1 lb mixed candied peel
* 2 lb moist sugar
* 2 lb chopped suet
* 2 oz mixed spices
* 1 teaspoon salt
* 16 eggs
* 1 gill brandy (¼ pint)
* 1 teaspoon lemon essence
* 1 teaspoon ratafia essence [almond essence]
* 1 tablespoon dried flour
* Milk at discretion

Cakes

To test if the cake is cooked, spike the cake with a skewer near the end of the suggested cooking time – if it comes out nice and clean, the cake is cooked and therefore remove from the oven to cool. If there is any liquid sponge on the end of the skewer, replace in the oven and cook for a further 5 minutes before testing again.

PATENT FLOUR

To each lb flour:

* 2 teaspoons cream of tartar
* 1 teaspoon soda
* 1 teaspoon sugar
* 1 teaspoonful salt

All ingredients separately dried and mixed, sift once or twice thoroughly and keep in a tin, dry.

AUNT CHARLEY'S TEA CAKE

* ½ lb flour
* 2 oz sugar
* 2 oz butter
* 1 egg
* 1 teaspoon cream of tartar
* ½ teaspoon bicarbonate of soda
* Milk

Rub the butter into the flour into which the cream of tartar and bicarbonate of soda have been previously well mixed. Beat up the egg with the sugar, add milk and make it very moist. Bake in cake tins very well greased. Bake in a quick oven for 15–20 minutes. Glaze with egg when baked. Scones as above but minus the egg and dough thick. Do not roll but pat out with hand to required shape. Much loved by children of all ages.

MRS SUTTON'S TEA CAKE

* 5 teacups flour
* 1 cup brown sugar
* 2 heaped teaspoons cream of tartar
* 1 heaped teaspoon bicarbonate of soda
* 2 eggs beaten together
* Milk to make all into a batter-like dough to pour

Put into a round tin and bake in a hot oven. Warm when required for tea and spread with butter.

SWEET SCONES (MRS MORLEY)

* ¾ lb flour
* ¼ lb butter
* 2 oz caster sugar
* 2 teaspoons baking powder
* 1 egg (beaten with milk)

Roll into 3 dumplings and cut each in 4, i.e. 12 in all.

TIRED HOUSEWIFE'S CAKE

- 1 lb flour
- ½ lb butter
- ½ lb sugar
- ½ lb sultanas
- ½ lb currants or other fruits desired
- 2 small teaspoons baking soda
- A little mixed peel
- 1 teaspoon each of vanilla, almond and lemon extract
- 1 teaspoon each of grated nutmeg, mixed spice and cinnamon
- ½ pint boiling milk
- 2 eggs

Put the soda into the flour, then the butter. Add the sugar, spices and fruit. Beat up the eggs well and add the milk. Then mix all together. Bake for 2 hours in a nice oven. When baked this cake is 5 lb in weight.

SPONGE CAKE

2 eggs and their weight in flour and a little less than their weight of sugar. 1 oz of baking powder. Mix the dry ingredients. Beat the eggs and add. Spread in 2 tins and bake in a quick oven. Sandwich with jam or butter cream.

EMILY CAMPBELL'S CHRISTMAS CAKE

* 1 lb butter or ½ margarine/½ butter
* 1 lb currants
* 1 lb sultanas
* 1 lb raisins
* ¼ lb mixed peel
* ¼ lb almonds
* 4 breakfast cups flour
* 2 heaped teaspoons baking powder
* 1 teaspoon cinnamon
* ½ teaspoon ground cloves
* 1 teaspoon mixed spice
* ½ teaspoon ground nutmeg
* 1 teaspoon each of vanilla, almond and lemon essence
* 1 wineglass brandy (or wine)
* 10 eggs
* 1 lb brown sugar

MARCHPANE (MARZIPAN)

Pound 8 units of almonds with 1 white of egg till smooth. Mix with 8 units of apricot preserve or any jam of the same consistency with no stones or seeds. Put into an enamelled pan, dust finely with powdered sugar and stir till dry enough to roll out or press into sugared moulds. This variously coloured and flavoured is the foundation of many French bonbons.

EGGLESS DATE CAKE (NATALIE)

- 1 cup milk
- ½ lb butter
- 1½ lb sugar
- 1 lb flour
- 1 lb dates
- 2 oz walnuts
- 2 teaspoons cocoa
- 2 teaspoons vinegar
- 2 teaspoons bicarbonate of soda

Dissolve the soda in 1 cup of milk. Cream the butter and sugar. Add the vinegar to the soda and milk mixture, lastly the dry ingredients. Mix well and bake in a flat tin till brown.

COCONUT WHISKS

* 2 oz butter
* 4 oz sugar
* 1 egg
* 2 heaped cups coconut (desiccated)

Cream the sugar and the butter. Add the beaten egg and then the coconut. Mix well and put small spoonfuls on a greased tray (leaving enough room for them to spread) and bake in the centre of the oven for 5–6 minutes. Wait 5 minutes before lifting them from the tray to cool on a wire rack.

GOOD FRUIT CAKE (NATALIE)

* 6 oz butter
* 6 oz sugar
* 4 eggs
* 1 tablespoon milk
* 2 cups flour
* 2 teaspoons baking powder
* 1½ cups fruit
* Vanilla essence

Cream the butter and sugar, then add the eggs, one by one, beating thoroughly. Add the milk, essence, flour and baking powder and fruit. Bake for 1½ hours

COLD OVEN FRUIT CAKE

This mixture makes a lovely big cake.

* ¾ lb butter
* ¾ lb sugar
* 1 teacup milk
* 1 teaspoon baking powder
* 1½ lb flour
* 6 tablespoons golden syrup
* 1 teaspoon salt
* 2 lb fruit (or more)
* 4 or 5 eggs
* Essence to taste (almond, vanilla, etc.)

Cream the butter and sugar together till light and fluffy. Sieve the baking powder, salt and flour into a separate bowl. Warm the milk and syrup in a saucepan, but do not boil. Beat the eggs. Add the fruit and essence and mix everything together. Put on the bottom shelf of the oven and turn the element on low and cook for 5 hours.

FRUIT CAKE 2

Beat ½ lb butter and ½ lb sugar to a cream. Add 4 eggs one by one. Add 2 tablespoons syrup, 1 tablespoon vinegar, ¼ teaspoon soda, ¾ lb flour mixing well together. Lastly, add ½ lb sultanas, ½ lb currants, ½ cup almonds, ½ cup candied cherries, dessertspoon powdered ginger.

MRS INGRAM'S SPONGE

Melt a nut of butter in 3 tablespoons of milk and pour on 3 eggs beaten with 6 oz of sugar. Beat well. Then add 4 oz of flour and a teaspoon of baking powder.

ARROWROOT SPONGE (MRS PALMER)

- 3 eggs
- ¾ breakfast cup sugar
- 1 good tablespoon flour
- 1 good tablespoon arrowroot
- 1 teaspoon baking powder
- Grated rind of 1 orange (use juice for filling and icing)
- You can leave orange out and use coconut

Beat the eggs for 5 minutes by the clock adding the sugar gradually and beat for another 5 minutes by the clock. Fold in the arrowroot, orange rind, flour and baking powder which have been previously mixed and sieved several times. Bake in a moderate oven for about ¾ hour.

THREE MINUTE SPONGE (RAPA)

* 1 breakfast cup flour
* 1 teacup sugar
* 2 oz melted butter
* Pinch of salt
* 2 eggs
* 1 heaped teaspoon baking powder

ORANGE CAKE 1

* Milk to mix
* 6 oz butter
* 8 oz flour
* 8 oz sugar
* 3 eggs
* 1 teaspoon heaped baking powder
* Pinch of salt
* Juice and grated rind of 1 orange or of 2 passion fruit

Cream the butter and sugar, add the yolks of the eggs one at a time. Add the whites (beaten stiffly), rind of orange (grated) and juice. Add the flour and baking powder. Add the milk to make it fairly runny. Have the oven so that the doorknob is not too hot to touch. Place 1 tray at the top with a pan of cold water on it. Place the cake on a shelf 3 places down. Bake for about 1 hour. Cake should rise evenly, bubbles on top – leave the front of stove open for the last quarter of an hour. Add very little fuel. Take the water out after about ½ hour if the cake has not browned on top.

When quite cold, cover with the following icing:

* Dessertspoon of butter
* Juice half an orange
* Cup icing sugar

Cream the butter and sugar and add the orange juice and then more icing sugar till stiff. 1 tablespoon of thick cream instead of butter if preferred with a little orange rind on top.

For chocolate cake – 2 tablespoons of cocoa, dissolved in ½ a cup of water.

ORANGE CAKE 2

* 3 oz butter
* 3 oz caster sugar
* 1 teacup milk
* 2 eggs
* 5 oz flour

Beat the butter to a cream, add the sugar, the yolks well beaten, milk and dredge in the flour. Beat well, then add the whites of the eggs well whisked. Spread equal quantities on three plates and bake to a delicate brown.

FILLING FOR ORANGE CAKE

This mix should be prepared first before the cake.

* 1 lemon
* 2 oranges
* 1 teacup sugar
* 1 teacup water
* 1 tablespoon cornflour

Grate the rind of the lemon and oranges and strain the juice. Wet the cornflour with the water and add the sugar. Add this to the rinds and juice. Boil for a few minutes, stirring well, then allow it to get quite cool. Spread on the cake which should be quite cold. Place together and sprinkle with a little caster sugar.

COCONUT WHISKS

* 2 oz butter
* 4 oz sugar
* Add 1 egg
* ½ teaspoonful vanilla essence
* 2 heaped cups coconut

Pour small spoonfuls on a greased tray and bake in very moderate oven.

CORNFLAKE CRISPS

Cream ¼ lb of butter and 3 oz of sugar. Crumble 2 cups of cornflakes, 1 ½ cups of flour, a pinch of salt, 1 teaspoon of cream of tartar. Dissolve ½ teaspoon of soda in ¼ cup of boiling water and add to the other ingredients. Mix to a dough and roll out thinly and cut into squares. Bake in a moderate oven till light brown.

WHOLEMEAL CAKE (MRS MACLAREN)

* ½ lb butter
* ½ lb sugar
* 1 teaspoon baking powder
* ¾ lb wholemeal and ordinary flour (½ and ½)
* 3 eggs
* Grated rind and juice of orange, essence of almonds and lemon

Slow oven 2 hours.

CHOCOLATE CAKE (JANET LORIMER)

* 6 oz butter
* 6 oz sugar
* 8 oz flour
* 3 eggs
* 2 teaspoons cream of tartar*
* 1 teaspoon soda*
* 2 dessertspoons cocoa
* Water

Beat the butter and sugar to a cream, add the eggs, then the cocoa made with ¾ cup of boiling water. Add flour and rising*. Cook for about ½ hour in a moderate oven.

ANGEL CAKE

- Whites of 5 eggs
- 1½ oz cornflour
- 1½ oz flour
- ½ teaspoon baking powder
- Pinch salt
- 5 oz caster sugar
- Vanilla extract
- ½ teaspoon cream of tartar

Sift the flour, cornflour, salt, cream of tartar and baking powder together. Whisk whites stiffly, stir in the sugar and dry ingredients, add the vanilla last. Bake for 15 minutes in a moderate oven for ¾ hour. When well risen, cover with a piece of greaseproof paper to prevent it from browning. Allow it to cool in the tin before removing on to a plate.

GINGER BREAD 1 (MRS CURRIE)

* 1 cup each of butter, milk, cream, treacle, sugar
* 4 cups flour
* 1 level tablespoon soda (bicarbonate)
* Spices, a little of everything: teaspoon cinnamon, mixed spice, nutmeg, ginger
* 1 tablespoon cocoa
* Flat, large cake tin

GINGER BREAD 2 (MISS GRAY)

* 3 cups flour
* 1 cup brown sugar
* ¼ lb butter
* ½ packet mixed spice
* 1 tablespoon ground ginger
* 2 teaspoons soda
* 1 cup boiling water
* ½ cup golden syrup
* Dried fruit and mixed peel

Cream the butter and sugar, add the flour and spices. Then bring the golden syrup and water to the boil and mix in the soda first with the boiling liquid, then the fruit and mixed peel.

ROCK CAKES 1

* 4 units butter
* 4 units sugar
* 16 units flour
* 8 units currants and sultanas, mixed
* 2 units candied peel
* Lemon peel
* 4 units eggs
* A little milk

Mix together. The paste must be very stiff. Using a dessertspoon, place rough, rocky lumps on to a greased baking sheet and dust with caster sugar.

ROCK CAKES 2

* 3 heaped up tablespoons flour
* 1½ heaped up tablespoons butter
* 1½ flat tablespoons sugar
* 2 flat tablespoons chopped fruits or peel
* 1 egg (beaten)
* 2 tablespoons milk or enough to make the dough hold together.

20 minutes moderate oven.

SWISS ROLL

* 5 units flour
* 5 units sifted sugar
* ⅛ unit baking powder
* 6 units eggs

Beat the yolks and sugar, dredge in the flour and add the stiffly frothed whites. Bake in a shallow tin – the sponge should not be more than ½ inch when cooked. Turn on to a dry clean cloth while sponge still hot and spread with hot jam. Roll up.

GINGER CAKE (MRS CAHUSAC)

* 1 lb flour
* 4 oz demerara sugar
* 4 oz butter
* 12 oz treacle
* 2 oz ginger
* 1 teaspoon bicarbonate of soda
* 4 eggs

Put the treacle, sugar and butter into a saucepan and stir over a low fire until the whole has melted. Take off the fire and add the flour, ginger, bicarbonate of soda and 2 eggs by degrees. Mix the whole together until it looks like a smooth paste, then add the remaining 2 eggs. Put in a tin that has been lined with buttered paper and bake.

SWISS CAKES

* 4 eggs plus their weight in:
* Butter, flour and sugar
* Grated lemon zest or 10 drops lemon essence [recipe page 39]
* 1 large teaspoon rosewater

Beat the egg yolks with the sugar and lemon zest or essence, then add the rosewater. Melt the butter and add to the mixture, then the flour, beating it well. Whisk the whites till softly stiff and add. Butter a tin and bake for 1 hour.

VINEGAR CAKE

Rub 1 lb flour into ½ lb butter. Add ½ lb sugar, ½ lb currants, ½ lb sultanas, 2 oz candied peel, chopped fine.

Put ¼ pint of milk into a large jug then 3 tablespoons of vinegar. Mix in a cup 1 teaspoonful of bicarbonate of soda with a little milk and put into the milk and vinegar. It will effervesce. Mix the cake quickly and put into a nice hot oven for the first ½ hour, then moderate the heat till done. This quantity will make 2 cakes. Moist brown sugar is best and margarine does really splendidly instead of butter. The cake is made preferably in one as it keeps better.

WHITE CAKE

Beat and cream ½ cup of butter with 1 cup of sugar. Add ½ cup of milk, 1½ cups of flour, vanilla essence. Lastly, add the whites of 3 eggs, stiffly whisked.

FROSTING FOR WHITE CAKE

Boil together 1 cup of sugar and ¼ cup of water till it strings. Add the sugar syrup to whisked whites of 1 or 2 eggs in a constant stream, whisking continuously until the mixture thickens and is almost cold. Quickly pour the icing over the cake and spread with a knife. This will have a crust on the surface but will be soft underneath unlike Royal icing which dries rock hard. Can be varied indefinitely. Chopped figs and walnuts mixed in is excellent – or banana or raisins, orange, etc. The same quantity will do one or two whites.

GLACE ICING

To every 2 units of white sugar just 1 of water. Boil for 1 minute, set to cool, stirring vigorously. Add any flavour desired. The syrup will soon begin to get cloudy, then opaque. Seize the intermediate stage, when it is fairly cloudy but still liquid and use it to mask cakes, genoises, pastry, etc. Curaçao, noyaux may be used as flavouring. If lemon is desired, take for an icing 8 units of sugar, as much tartaric or citric acid as will lie on a 2 anna bit. Wet with a drop or two of water and lemon essence and stir the whole in the syrup when it begins to get cloudy, not before. The syrup will never harden if not stirred, but the above proportions cannot fail with 1 minute's boiling.

CREAM ICING

Boil 10 units of thick cream and sugar together as for cream toffee. When fairly thick stir it into a sufficiency of finely powdered white sugar to make the whole a stiff paste. Add flavouring and colouring if desired while still warm. Arrange over the cake using a biscuit forcer for the purpose. Coffee cream icing only requires the addition of a little essence of coffee while the cream and sugar are being boiled.

CREAM TOFFEE

Boil 10 units of white sugar with 5 units of cream until the bottom of the pan shows distinctly in the stirring. Add vanilla and pour into an oiled tin.

COCONUT ICE

* 6 units pounded sugar
* 3 units water
* 6 units grated coconut

Boil the sugar and water for 1 minute. Set to cool stirring vigorously. The syrup will soon get cloudy, then opaque. Seize the intermediate state when it is fairly cloudy, not still liquid. Mix in the coconut quickly and pour into an oiled dry dish. Take the same proportion of sugar and water as before, add cochineal, stir till cloudy and pour over the white ice. When firm, cut with a sharp knife.

RUSSIAN TOFFEE (MRS CAHUSAC)

* 1 lb 4 oz demerara sugar*
* ½ lb butter
* 1 breakfast cup cream, heaped

Put all into a saucepan together and boil till it balls. (*i.e. about 2 heaped breakfast cups of sugar and 12 oz of cream).

BURNT ALMONDS

* 8 units No. 3 Shahjehanpur sugar or chini
* 4 units milk

Melt over a done fire and add 4 units of baked almonds, well browned in the oven, stirring with a bamboo twig whisk. The sugar should adhere to the almonds and get quite dry.

CHOCOLATE CREAMS

Mix 2 units of arrowroot smoothly with 3 units of cold water. Add 12 of powdered sugar, boil rapidly for 8–10 minutes stirring continuously. Remove from the fire and stir till a little cool. Flavour with vanilla or rose. Continue stirring till it creams, then roll into little balls. Melt some chocolate over steam, adding no water, and when the cream balls are cold, roll them in it one by one. Lay on a buttered slab to cool. The creams may be varied by dividing into 3 parts, adding grated coconut to one, chopped almonds to another and pistachios to the third. By decreasing the water slightly and adding a little melted butter this makes a good icing for cakes.

CARAMEL FUDGE (MRS HARRIS)

* 2 cups sugar
* ⅔ cup milk
* 3 tablespoons butter
* Water

Put the milk and 1½ cups of sugar in a pan and boil for 8 minutes. Caramelise the remaining sugar with a dessertspoon of water and add to the milk and boil till it will set in cold water. Take off the heat and add the butter, beating. Pour into a greased mould. Have the milk and sugar boiling very well before adding the caramel. Very good.

GINGER ROCK

* 8 units white sugar
* 1 unit ground ginger
* 2 units butter
* 3 units water

Boil as for toffee.

Biscuits, Breads and Buns

CHEESE SCONES (MRS CHILD'S RECIPE)

* 1 breakfast cup grated cheese
* 2 breakfast cups flour
* 4 teaspoons baking powder
* 1 teaspoonful salt
* 1 breakfast cup milk (more or less)
* 1 tablespoon butter

Mix and sift the dry ingredients, rub in the butter and the cheese. Mix in the milk slowly. Flatten, and cut into shape and put a small piece of butter on top of each scone. Hot oven for 10–15 minutes. Excellent.

OATMEAL SCONES

* 6 tablespoons oatmeal or 2 Quaker Oats
* 6 tablespoons flour
* 3 tablespoons sugar
* 1 chittack butter
* 2 eggs well beaten
* ½ breakfast cup sour milk
* 1 level teaspoon bicarbonate of soda
* 1 level teaspoon cream of tartar
* 1 level teaspoon Yeatman's baking powder

Mix the flour, oatmeal, sugar, etc. Rub in the butter. Add the eggs, lastly the sour milk. Make into scones and bake.

BREAKFAST SCONES

To 1 lb of flour add 1 teaspoon of baking powder. Enough buttermilk to make into a stiff dough. Make it into scones and bake.

POTATO SCONES

* 16 units mashed potato
* 1 unit butter
* 1 egg yolk
* Some salt
* 8 units flour

Mix the potato with the butter, egg yolk, some salt and add the flour. If necessary, add a little milk to moisten. Roll out as thin as possible and cut into rounds and toast or bake on a griddle. Serve as muffins.

CHEESE BISCUITS 1

* ¼ lb fresh butter
* ¼ lb flour
* 5 oz rich cheese, grated
* 1 teaspoonful dry mustard powder
* 6 salt spoons cayenne pepper
* Yolks 2 eggs, well beaten
* 2 tablespoons cold water

Beat the butter to a cream, add the flour, cheese, mustard, cayenne, water and yolks. Mix well, knead to a fine paste and roll it out ⅛ inch thick. Cut into biscuits with a circular cutter about 2 inches in diameter or cut into slices 1 inch wide and 3 inches long. Bake in a quick oven. Serve very hot.

CHEESE BISCUITS 2 (MRS MACLAREN)

* 1½ breakfast cups flour
* 2 oz butter
* Salt
* 4 oz dry grated cheese
* ½ teaspoon baking powder
* ½ cup milk

Make a dough neither too wet nor too dry.

WATER BISCUITS

- ¼ lb flour
- Pinch of salt
- 2 tablespoons water
- ½ oz butter

Sieve the salt and flour. Melt the butter and water and pour it into the flour mixing well. Roll out very thinly, cut into rounds and prick with a fork. Bake. Sprinkle with a little salt and store in an airtight tin.

BROWN BREAD 1

1. 1 yeast cake broken up and mixed with ½ cup of wholemeal, 1 tablespoon of brown sugar, a little warm water to make into a paste (not runny). Leave to rise for about ½ hour.

2. 10 cups of flour flat, 1 flat tablespoon of salt, mix in the risen yeast a little and add hottish water (about 2 pints or a little less). Mix well and leave to rise about ½ hour.

3. Knead for 10 minutes on a floured board. Form into loaves. Set aside to rise again for ½ to ¾ hour. Cook in a brisk oven for ½ hour.

BROWN BREAD 2

- 16 units wholemeal flour
- ¼ unit bicarbonate of soda
- ¼ unit salt
- 14 units cream of tartar
- 20 units milk or milk/water

Mix the soda and salt well with the flour, sifting twice. Dissolve the cream of tartar in milk (or milk/water), mix rapidly but thoroughly. Bake in a sharp oven for 1 hour.

PULLED BREAD

Take the crust off a new, warm loaf. Pull the crumb into rough pieces about 2 inches long. Lay them on a sheet of paper on a baking tray. Bake in slow oven till crisp through and golden brown. Serve with butter and cheese.

MALT BISCUITS

* 1 cup butter
* ¾ cup sugar
* 4 cups flour
* 1 tablespoon cocoa
* 1 tablespoon full malt
* 2 eggs
* Pinch of salt
* 1 teaspoon bicarbonate of soda

Cream the butter and sugar, add the beaten eggs, malt and other ingredients. Very stiff mixture. Shape and let stand overnight or for 2 hours wrapped in greaseproof paper. Roll out thin and cut into rounds. Bake on a cold greased tray in a moderate oven for 20 minutes.

BRAN BISCUITS

* ¼ lb butter
* ¼ cup sugar
* 2 cups flour
* 2 cups bran
* 2 teaspoons baking powder
* Milk
* 1 egg

Cream the butter and sugar, add the egg and a little milk and the remaining ingredients. Roll out.

RUSKS

- ½ lb flour
- 3 oz butter
- ½ teaspoon baking powder
- Pinch of salt

Roll out to almost ¼ inch and cut into rounds. Put in a hot oven to rise and when half cooked spilt in two. Replace in the oven and continue cooking at a reduced heat (with door slightly ajar) to brown – a further 5–8 minutes.

FANNY'S CAKES (MY 3 X GREAT-GRANDMOTHER FANNY CHARLOTTE CAMPBELL)

- 2 oz butter
- 2 oz sugar
- 2 oz fat almonds

WALNUT BREAD (MRS SHALLARD)

* 3 cups flour
* ¾ cup brown sugar
* 3 teaspoons baking powder
* 1 egg
* 1 cup milk
* 2 oz butter
* 1 cup walnuts
* ½ tablespoon golden syrup
* Pinch of salt

Mix the dry ingredients together. Cream the butter and sugar, mix in the syrup and beaten egg. Add the dry ingredients, chopped walnuts and lastly the milk to make a very stiff dough. Bake for 1 hour in a moderate oven.

DATE LOAF (MRS SHALLARD)

* 2 heaped cups flour
* Small cup sugar
* 3 tablespoons butter
* 1 cup dates
* Small drop vanilla
* 1 teaspoon baking soda
* Water

Soak dates in one cup of boiling water, add soda and vanilla. Beat butter and sugar to a cream, add dates and egg mixture and lastly, flour. 1 teaspoon cream of tartar added. Bake for 1 hour.

SHORT CRUST PASTRY FOR SWEET TARTS

* 1 lb flour
* ½ lb butter
* ¼ lb sugar
* 2 yolks of egg
* 1 teacup milk and water mixed

Mix all together to a paste.

DROP SCONES

* 2 teacups flour
* 2 tablespoons caster sugar
* 1 teaspoon bicarbonate of soda
* ½ teaspoon tartaric acid
* 1 egg
* A little buttermilk

Mix all the dry ingredients together, then add the egg and the buttermilk and mix with a wooden spoon and beat well and make into a thick batter. Leave to stand for 5 minutes, when the surface should be covered by air cells. Cook on a griddle or butter a frying pan and cook, not fry in that, keeping the scones as round as possible.

PIKELETS

* Heaped breakfast cup flour
* Heaped teaspoon baking powder
* 1 tablespoon sugar
* Butter size of large walnut
* 1 or 2 eggs
* Milk

Mix dry ingredients together. Rub in the butter. One or two eggs well beaten in milk to make a good consistency, drop. Fry pan or griddle. Drop from top of a tablespoon. When the third is dropped, the first is ready to turn. Insert the blade of a knife directly in the centre of a pikelet and turn over.

GINGER SNAPS (RAPA)

Melt 2 oz of butter with 1 tablespoon of golden syrup and 1½ tablespoons of sugar. Add 2 oz of flour, ½ teaspoon of baking powder, pinch of salt, 1 teaspoon of ground ginger and vanilla essence. Put on a tray in about ½ teaspoonful lumps. Bake slowly in moderate oven.

BUNS

* 1 lb flour
* 6 oz butter
* 2 teaspoons baking powder
* ¼ lb sugar
* 1 egg
* Nearly ¼ pint milk
* Essence of lemon

Mix together all the above ingredients and shape into buns (makes 24). Bake in a moderately hot oven. Currants and/or raisins may be added.

CORNFLOUR BUNS

Beat together 1 oz of butter and 2 oz of sugar to a cream. Add 1 egg and 3 oz of flour and 1oz of cornflour beaten in enough milk to make a fairly thin batter. Few currants or grated lemon peel or finely cut candied peel beaten in. Finally add a small teaspoon of baking powder. Makes 12 buns.

MACAROONS (MOTHER'S [FANNY CHARLOTTE CAMPBELL])

½ lb almonds pounded in a mortar (a little beaten white of egg to be added while pounding to prevent oiling). Beat in by degrees 8 chittacks of caster sugar and beaten up white of egg till the proper consistency. Bake on sheets of paper a light brown.

WALNUT MACAROONS

As above recipe. The walnuts however only want to be roughly crumbled and no white of egg is used in crushing. Walnuts should be peeled. Most excellent.

BATTER

Mix 4 oz of sifted flour, salt and pepper with 2 tablespoons of salad oil to a stiff paste. This should be made several hours in advance. 10 minutes before use whip the whites of 2 eggs to a stiff froth and beat them in lightly.

Preserves, Jams and Chutneys

MRS SHALLARD'S WAY OF BOTTLING FRENCH BEANS

Top and tail and string young fresh beans. Put in a bowl and pour boiling water over them. Leave for 8 minutes. Pour the water away and cover with cold water for a minute. Fill your wide-mouthed jars with the beans (cut up if you wish, or whole, which looks better) and make a solution of cooled boiled water and to each quart of water add 1 oz of sugar and ½ oz of salt. Add a dessertspoonful of vinegar to each quart jar. Put the lids on after having filled with the cool boiled water and boil for 2 hours then let them stand for 24 hours and then boil again for 1 hour. In taking out for the second time put on the rubbers and be sure your boiling liquid is filled to overflowing.

GREEN GOOSEBERRY MARMALADE

- 3 lb gooseberries
- 3 lemons
- 6 breakfast cups water
- 6 lb sugar

Slice or mince the lemons. Cover with 3 cups of boiling water, stand for 12 hours. Place in a preserving pan with the gooseberries and the last 3 cups of water. Boil for 1 hour. Add the warmed sugar, boil quickly for 30 minutes. Bottle and seal while hot. This is a delicious marmalade with a lovely colour.

GOOSEBERRY CHUTNEY

- 1½ pints green gooseberries
- ¼ lb raisins
- 1 tablespoon salt
- 1 teaspoonful mustard seed
- 6 oz brown sugar
- 2 onions
- 2 oz sultanas
- 1 teaspoonful ground ginger
- Pinch of cayenne pepper
- A good pinch of turmeric

Wash, top and tail the gooseberries and cut in half. Put all the ingredients into an enamelled pan. Bring slowly up to the boil, simmer for about 1 hour, stirring often. Put into hot, sterilised jars and cover.

GUAVA JELLY AND CHEESE (MRS JOHNSON, KOHAT 1898)

Wash and slice guavas and put into a jar. To 6 seers of guavas add 2 breakfast cups of water. Seal down and simmer for about 5 hours – or until the guavas are quite soft. Then strain through a big coarse gharam and, while the pulp is still hot, rub it through a very coarse gharam or sieve.

Cheese: To each seer of juice put 1 seer of No. 2 sugar and 3 chittacks of lime juice. Boil till it leaves the sides of the pan. Oil paper with salad oil and line a tin and pour the cheese.

APPLE CHUTNEY

- ✻ 5 lb green apples
- ✻ 1 lb raisins
- ✻ 2 lb sultanas
- ✻ 4 oz green ginger
- ✻ 1 oz garlic
- ✻ 1 lb sugar
- ✻ 1 quart vinegar
- ✻ 1 tablespoon salt
- ✻ ½ powdered chillies
- ✻ 4 oz mustard seed

Peel and core the apples and cut in slices. Wash the raisins. Peel and cut up the ginger and the garlic and pound to a pulp in a mortar. Boil the sugar with ½ the quart of vinegar to a thick syrup. Lay the cut apples on a dish, cover with ½ the salt and let stand for 15 hours or all night.

When the apples have stood long enough, boil in the remaining vinegar till tender but do not mash them. Let the apples get cold, then add the syrup (cold) and all the other ingredients including the remainder of the salt.

Pour into hot, sterilised jars and seal securely. Let the chutney stand for 5 or 6 weeks before using.

G A Croly

APRICOT OR PEACH CHUTNEY

There are many other kinds of chutneys made by boiling fruit pulp with sugar till it is thick, then adding vinegar, salt, raisins, spices. The proportions generally are:

* 16 units fruit pulp
* 12 units vinegar
* 8 units raisins
* Salt, ginger, chillies and garlic according to fancy

EMERGENCY CHUTNEY 1

A very good 'chutney' can be made by mixing 2–3 tablespoons of any fruit jam (apricot and plum are particularly successful) with 1–2 tablespoons of Worcestershire sauce.

EMERGENCY CHUTNEY 2

Another very good chutney can be quickly prepared by using any acid jam such as blackcurrant, damson or plum. Put the jam into a basin and mix with it the following ingredients to taste: vinegar, salt, powdered chillies, pounded green ginger, sultanas, almonds (blanched and finely sliced) and if liked, a little pounded garlic. Stir well together and bottle. It does not need to be boiled.

MINT JELLY

A delicious jelly to have with cold meats can be made by preparing some mint sauce and adding 1 dessertspoonful of gelatine to every cup of liquid. Have the liquid warm enough to dissolve the gelatine.

MANGO CHUTNEY

64 units of (solid) green mangoes, sliced. Sprinkle with salt and set in the sun for 24 hours. Drain and boil with 20 units of vinegar till tender. Boil 20 more units of vinegar with 16 units of sugar and stir into it 16 units of pulped, dried apricots, 8 units of almonds and 8 units of ground ginger, 4 units each of garlic, red chillies and mustard seed – all ground. Add to the mangoes and set in the sun.

KASHMIR CHUTNEY

* 2 lb brown sugar
* ½ lb green ginger
* ½ lb garlic
* ¼ lb white mustard seed
* 6 oz raisins
* 2 oz dried chillies
* 1 quart vinegar

Boil the sugar with half the vinegar to a syrup. Pound the other ingredients and mix with the syrup and the remainder of the vinegar.

Put the chutney into a large jar and keep in a warm dry place for a fortnight, stirring every day. It will then be ready to bottle and fasten down.

FRUIT PICKLE

Take equal quantities of dried dates, prunes, fresh apples such as pippins, dried plums, dried apricots. Wash all the fruits thoroughly and dry carefully. Soften the dates by stewing gently for about ¼ hour. Remove the date pips and cut into slices. Cut the apples into quarters, rings or any fancy shape. Arrange the mixed fruit in bottles, with a few peppercorns, some cinnamon sticks, a few slices of ginger and a little salt. Boil a ¼ lb of sugar with a ¼ pint of vinegar and pour hot over the bottled fruit. After the fruit swells a little more of the sugar and vinegar may be added. The fruit should be completely covered and the bottles full. Cover and stand for a month before using.

MINT CHUTNEY

Take a couple of bunches of mint and bash to a pulp in a mortar, then place in a saucer and sprinkle it with salt. Squeeze the juice of a lemon over it. Cut up an onion and a couple of green chillies, then mix the whole. Serve with curry and rice.

CUCUMBER RELISH

* 1½ lb cucumber
* 1 onion finely chopped
* ¼ lb sugar
* ½ tablespoon salt
* 2 small cups vinegar
* 1 lb apples green
* ½ teaspoon cayenne

Put the vinegar, salt, sugar, cayenne and apple (minced) on to boil till the apple is soft. Leave to cool. Add the minced cucumber and onion. Do not peel the cucumber but wash and quarter lengthways removing the seeds.

FRESH TOMATO CHUTNEY

* 3 large ripe tomatoes
* 1 teaspoonful sugar
* 1 dessertspoon vinegar
* ½ teaspoonful salt
* ½ teaspoonful powdered chillies

Bake the tomatoes in the oven till they split, peel and core them, break up the pulp thoroughly and add the vinegar, sugar, salt and powdered chillies.

PEAS PRESERVED UNDERGROUND

Simply shell good sound peas, pack them as tightly into jars as they go without bruising them. Seal well and bury 4 ft underground. This excludes all air and they will keep almost indefinitely.

ORANGE JELLY (MRS SHALLARD)

Slice 6 oranges and 2 lemons. Add 6 pints of water. Let it stand overnight, then boil till pulpy. Strain through a jelly bag. To every cup of juice add a cup of sugar. Boil for about an hour or until it jells.

MRS SHALLARD'S MARMALADE

To every 3 lb of cut fruit put 5 lb of sugar. To every lb of sugar put 1 gill of water.

Put the oranges whole into a saucepan and cover with cold water. Let them boil till soft changing the water after 1½ hours boiling. The oranges must be perfectly soft so that the head of a pin will pierce the fruit easily. Cut up the oranges into small pieces or slices taking out the pips. Put the sugar and water into a saucepan and let it boil for 8 or 10 minutes till the syrup is clear. Then put in the fruit. Stir well and boil for 40 minutes or a little longer. Excellent.

GOLDEN SHRED MARMALADE

- 3 Seville oranges and
- 3 sweet oranges or
- 6 sweet oranges if preferred
- 4 large lemons
- Sugar
- Water

Cut the outside off half the oranges into shreds, measuring 2 cups. Place in a basin and cover with water. Cut up roughly the remaining oranges. Keep the pips in a separate basin and cover with water.

Place the oranges in a preserving pan and cover with water, using 2 cups of water to every cup of orange. Add lemon juice and allow to stand overnight. Next day bring to the boil slowly and boil steadily for about 2 hours.

Add water and jelly from the pips as soon as the jam is hot. Boil shreds in a separate pan till tender. Test the liquid for pectin, and if ready strain through a jelly bag. Measure the liquid and return to a clean preserving pan. While hot add 1 cup of crystal sugar to every cup of juice. When the sugar has dissolved add the shreds and boil steadily without stirring for 20 minutes or until it sets when tested on a cold saucer.

Pour into jars when it has cooled. If bottled when hot the shreds rise to the surface. After bottling these may be distributed more evenly in the jelly by using a knitting needle. When cold, cover and seal.

GOOSEBERRY PRESERVE

* 1 lb green gooseberries
* 1¼ lb sugar

Top and tail the gooseberries and wash in cold water. Half cover with water and scald the fruit until it is soft. Add the sugar to the hot mixture. Bring quickly to boiling point and cook quickly until clear. Seal at once in clean, hot jars.

CAPE GOOSEBERRY JAM

* 4 lb cape gooseberries
* 1 lb apples

Peel, core and slice the apples thinly. Put in a pan with the gooseberries (no water). Sweat in the oven with the lid on till liquid. Boil on top of the stove till the fruit is quite cooked. Add 4 lb of sugar. When dissolved boil hard till jam jells. This makes just over 5 lb of jam and sets well.

QUINCE CONSERVE 1

Cover quinces with cold water. Boil till quite soft and let it rest. Peel quinces and cut into squares. Chop up the cores and boil with the skins a little longer, then strain through a cloth. To each cup of quince allow 3 cups of quince water and 3 cups of sugar. Boil the sugar and water together for a few minutes and then add the cut up quinces. Boil quickly till it jells.

QUINCE CONSERVE 2 (ENID LORIMER'S)

From each lb of quinces reserve 1 quince. Cut up the rest finely, skins and cores included and cook till soft. I put in quite a lot of water and cooked slowly with the lid on till the fruit was soft and yellowish. Strain off the juice and measure. Peel, core and cut up small the reserved quinces and cook in the juice till soft and coloured. Add 1 lb of sugar for each pint of juice and cook till it jells. I kept the lid on except when the sugar was in and made 2 pints of juice from 3 lb of quinces (less 3 quinces reserved), 2 lb of sugar and just over 3 lb of conserve.

PRESERVING PEEL

Quarter orange and lemon peel after having washed them thoroughly and removed all trace of pulp. Put them to soak, covered with water and about 1 tablespoon of salt. Let stand for a couple of days. Then boil in the same liquid till quite tender. Make a syrup of 2 cups of sugar to 1 cup of water (according to the amount required). Put the peel into the syrup and let it stand for a week, making sure that every bit of the peel is under the syrup. Boil in the syrup till clarified. Turn out of the syrup, let stand to dry till the syrup is all dried off. Coat with sugar and store away in screw top jars.

Beverages and Cocktails

ICE CUBE COFFEE

Make coffee as usual only double the strength – use 2 heaped tablespoons of coffee to each cup (½ pint) of water.

Pour the freshly made coffee into an ice cube tray and freeze. (A tray of these coffee cubes can be kept for instant use.) Now when iced coffee is wanted, simply heat milk. Do not bring the milk to a boil and do not use cream.

Fill a glass with the frozen coffee cubes. Then fill with warm milk – instantly you have a delicious, refreshing iced coffee of a consistency similar to iced coffee served with expensive cream.

ICED COFFEE

Take 8 oz of coffee to a quart of water. Place the coffee in a muslin bag and tie it up loosely. Boil up the water in an enamel pan, add the coffee and bring up to boiling point. Remove from the fire and allow the coffee bag to remain in the saucepan till cold. Beat 2 eggs very light, stir to them 1 pint of milk and ½ pint of cream. Mix with the coffee and stand in a refrigerator for 6 hours. Serve with ice in the jug and a dessertspoon of whipped cream.

MILK PUNCH (MRS SANDEEP)

* 1 dozen quarts rum
* 4 seers No. 1 sugar
* 6 seers milk
* 100 thin skinned limes
* ½ nutmeg (if liked, but Mrs S does not use it)

Peel the limes very finely and soak the skins in 3 bottles of rum for 36 hours. Then strain off the rum and mix it with the remaining 9 bottles of rum, 1 (rum) bottle of the lime and rum juice and 4 seers of sugar. Stir it all up well and add 6 seers of good fresh boiling milk. Let all this mixture stand for at least 24 hours well covered up. Then strain through flannel and bottle off. The great secret for getting it clear is for the milk to be boiling. Some people like the addition of ½ a powdered nutmeg. Mature for 6 months.

BARLEY WATER

* 4 large tablespoons pearl barley
* 8 lumps sugar
* The rind of 2 lemons and if liked, a little of the juice
* 1 quart boiling water

Put the barley in a saucepan with water to cover it. Bring it to the boil, then let it boil for 5 minutes. Next strain off the water and throw it away. (By doing this you remove the slightly bitter flavour of the barley and improve both the colour and the flavour of the barley water.) Next put the barley in a jug with the thinly pared rind of the lemons and the sugar. Pour on the boiling water. Cover the jug tightly and leave it until cold, then strain off the liquid into a clean jug and serve as cold as possible.

LEMON BARLEY WATER

Take 2 tablespoons of pearl barley, 4 oz of sugar, 2 quarts of boiling water and the peel of a fresh lemon. Let it stand all night, strain and serve as cold as possible.

MINT JULEP

Put a small bunch of fresh mint into a glass tumbler, add a tablespoon of white sugar, ½ a wineglass of peach brandy and the same of common brandy. Fill up with crushed ice.

MINT BEER

Put some fresh, bruised mint into a jug and pour over it a well-iced bottle of beer and a well-iced bottle of sparkling lemonade. Serve in glass tankards or tumblers.

FLASH

Mix ½ pint of lemon ice with a wineglass of rum. Pour over it, while stirring briskly, a bottle of iced ginger beer. Drink while it is effervescing.

POOR MAN'S CHAMPAGNE

Pour a pint of ale into a jug half filled with ice cubes and add a chilled bottle of ginger beer. Stir and serve immediately.

SUBSTITUTE FOR WINE

Take any fruit juice, put in 1 tablespoon of barley and put in a nice warm spot for 24 hours. Then drain off after fermentation and use the wine over a trifle sponge.

ANDREW FUSE (GIVEN BY A FRIEND)

- Glass: champaigne [sic] glass smeared with lemon and dusted with sugar
- Base: equal parts: Benedictine, rye whisky, brandy, square gin

This should be mixed in an iced shaker.

Topping: suggest chilled dry ginger ale with coiled lemon and orange peel.

Note: This drink sounds vicious (and is) but it tastes very harmless. I once gave a teetotal maiden aunt four in quick succession telling her they were soft drinks. She cut me out of her will.

Index

Note: Page numbers in **bold** refer to photographs.

Allahabad 12
almond 139, 188, 198, 209–10
burnt almonds 188
marchpane (marzipan) 170
anchovy
anchovy sauce 42
excellent sauce for fish 50
fish balls 79
Harvey's sauce 36
potted meat 86
sauce piquante 2 44
walnut ketchup 37
Andrew fuse 223
angel cake 180
apple 58, 105, 211, 215
apple Charlotte 151
apple chutney 208
apricot
apricot chutney 209
fruit creams 145
arrowroot sponge (Mrs Palmer) 174
asparagus
asparagus with cream 133
iced sauce for asparagus 50
sauce for asparagus 49
aspic, lobster salad in aspic 81
aubergine, bringal burta 110, 114
Aunt Louisa (pudding) 142
baati (unleavened bread) 7
bacon
bacon and egg pie 119
beetroot as a full meal 128
imitation pâté de foie gras 86
oatmeal and bacon stuffing 57
puftaloons with bacon 133
rabbit pie 98
tomatoes à la Provençale 1 126
baked pudding 149
banana
banana jelly 154
banana puffs with mock cream 155
barley water 221
lemon barley water 222
batter 21, 130, 203
frying batter 21
sweet baked batter pudding 140
bean(s) 17
French beans à la Provençale 125
Mrs Shallard's way of bottling French beans 206
béchamel sauce 52
beef
beef baked with potatoes 99
beef roll 85
bubble and squeak 132
galantine of beef 84

Hindu's beef 85
potato pie 113
potted meat 86
spiced beef 84
beer, mint beer 222
Beeton, Mrs, *Directions for Cookery* 1851 36
beetroot as a full meal 128
Begbie, Alfred William 12
Begbie (née Campbell), Emily Frances Margaret 11, 13, **13**, 14
Emily Campbell's Christmas cake 170
Begbie, Colonel Francis Richard 11
Begbie (née Grant), Margaret Anna 12
beverages 219–23
Birch (née Begbie), Eleanor 'Nell' Geraldine 11, 13, 14, **14**
biscuits 191–203
bran biscuits 197
cheese biscuits 194
ginger snaps (rapa) 201
malt biscuits 197
water biscuits 195
black cap pudding 147
blancmange, Dutch blancmange (Mother's [Frances Charlotte Campbell]) 153
boiling 17
Bolst, Colonel 7
bouillabaisse 80
brain
brain patties 89
brains soufflé 107
bran biscuits 197
brandy 222, 223
brandy sauce for plum pudding 56
bread 191–203
bread sauce 52
brown bread 195–6
croustades (croutons) 134
making stale loaves fresh 18
pulled bread 196
walnut bread (Mrs Shallard) 199
see also toast
breadcrumbs
apple Charlotte 151
Aunt Louisa (pudding) 142
baked pudding 149
baked and stuffed fish 80
beef roll 85
breaded cutlets 92
Christmas pudding 162
coconut meringue for filling tartlets 150
croquettes 94
curried meatballs 90
fried whole eggs 119
galantine of beef 84
golden pudding 157
half-pay pudding 151
lemon pudding 160
stuffed tomatoes 126
stuffed tripe 106
tomatoes à la Provençale 3 127
tomatoes and parsley 125
breakfast scones 193
bream, plain baked fish 78
Britain 8
brown bread 195–6
bubble and squeak 132
buns 202
cornflour buns 202
see also tea cakes
burtas 110
bringal burta 114
egg burta 124
potato burta 114

cabbage
bubble and squeak 132
mess of pottage 63
mixed vegetable soup 67
stuffing for roast duck 1 57
cake fillings 177, 186
cakes 18–19, 21, 165–89
angel cake 180
arrowroot sponge (Mrs Palmer) 174
chocolate cake 176
chocolate cake (Janet Lorimer) 179
cold oven fruit cake 173
eggless date cake (Natalie) 171
Emily Campbell's Christmas cake 170
Fanny's cakes 198
fruit cake 2 173
ginger cake (Mrs Cahusac) 184
good fruit cake (Natalie) 172
Mrs Ingram's sponge 174
orange cake 176–7
rock cakes 182–3
sponge cake 169
Swiss cakes 184
three minute sponge 175
tired housewife's cake 169
white cake 185
wholemeal cake (Mrs Maclaren) 178
see also tea cakes
Calcutta 8
calf's liver, imitation pâté de foie gras 86
Campbell, Sir Alexander William, 4th Baronet of Barcaldine (Great Uncle Alick), great-uncle Alick's fish pie 72
Campbell (née Begbie), Frances ('Fanny') Charlotte 11–12, **12**, 14, 144, 198
Fanny's cakes 198
macaroons 202
Xmas plum pudding 163
Campbell, John Peter William 12, **12**
candied peel 141, 163, 169–70, 182, 183, 185, 202
preserved lemon peel 217
preserved orange peel 217
cape gooseberry jam 215
caramel fudge (Mrs Harris) 189
carrot 62, 96
cauliflower 132
cayenne salt 30
champagne
Andrew fuse 223
poor man's champagne 222
Charlotte, apple Charlotte 151
cheese
baked cheese 135
cheese biscuits 194
cheese ramekins 124
cheese scones (Mrs Child's recipe) 192
cheese toast 135
guava jelly and cheese 207
mixed vegetable soup 67
tomato soufflé 127
cheesecake, lemon cheesecake 160
chicken
chicken curry 102–3
chicken curry with fruit 105
chicken dumpode 98
chicken/duckling curry 104
country captain 106
mulligatawny soup 65
pilau (pellow) 100–1
potato pie 113
Child, Mrs, cheese scones 192
chitchkee curry 111

chittacks (weight/measure) 15
chocolate
chocolate cake 176
chocolate cake (Janet Lorimer) 179
chocolate cream 156
chocolate creams 188
chocolate pudding 146
Christmas pudding 162–3
Xmas plum pudding (Mother's [Frances Charlotte Campbell]) 163
chutney 205–17
apple chutney 208
apricot chutney 209
emergency chutney 1&2 209
fresh tomato chutney 212
gooseberry chutney 207
Kashmir chutney 210
mango chutney 210
mint chutney 211
peach chutney 209
claret jelly 153
cocktails 219–23
coconut (desiccated) 65, 102, 139, 150
coconut meringue for filling tartlets 150
coconut pudding 152
coconut whisks 172
coconut (grated) 188
coconut ice 187
coconut milk
fresh coconut milk 29
recipes using 88
coconut whisks 178
coffee 18
coffee junket 152
coffee mould 152
ice cube coffee 220
iced coffee 220
condiments 25–39
cooking tips 17–19
coriander 8
cornflake crisps 178
cornflour buns 202
country captain 106
cream 154
asparagus with cream 133
banana puffs with mock cream 155
chocolate cream 156
cream béchamel 53
cream icing 186
cream toffee 187
creamed ices for preserved fruit 144
crème supreme (Sophie Grisbach's recipe) 143
endive or lettuce with cream 131
fruit creams 145
rice creams 161
vanilla cream 155
croquettes 94
croustades (croutons) 134
pumpkin soup with croutons 68
cucumber 8, 64
cucumber maître d'hôtel 131
cucumber relish 212
cucumber with white sauce 131
sauce for cucumber salad 47
Cumberland sauce 44
currant(s) 141, 151, 162–3, 169–70, 173, 182, 185, 202
curry 7
chicken curry 102–3
chicken curry with fruit 105
chicken/duckling curry 104
chitchkee curry 111
curried meatballs 90
curry paste 27

dhal and egg curry 118
egg curry 117
fish curry 77
Madras curry powder 26
meat curry 87
meat curry with fruit 88
pork curry 97
prawn curry 73
vegetable curry 132
custard 21, 134
custard (Mother's [Frances Charlotte Campbell]) 144
orange custard 140
Princess Royal custard 139
tomato custards 127
vanilla cream 155

Dalvey 12
date(s) 211
date loaf (Mrs Shallard) 199
eggless date cake (Natalie) 171
Devil meat 93
Devil mixture 29
devilled eggs 122
dhal
dhal churchurree 116
dhal and egg curry 118
dhal pooree 115
kitcheree 1 111
rice and dhal 117
stewed dhal 114
dried fruit 183
Christmas pudding 162–3
cold oven fruit cake 173
dried fruit to stew 158
fruit cake 2 173
fruit pickles 211
rock cakes 182–3
see also currant(s); date(s); raisin(s); sultana(s)
drop scones 200
duck
chicken/duckling curry 104
orange salad for wild duck 135
sauce for wild duck 53–4
stuffing for roast duck 1 57–8
dumpode, chicken dumpode 98
Dutch blancmange (Mother's [Frances Charlotte Campbell]) 153

East India Company 12
egg 47, 50, 64, 124, 126
bacon and egg pie 119
batter 130
cakes 170, 173–4, 176, 178–80, 182–5
coconut meringue for filling tartlets 150
custard (Mother's [Frances Charlotte Campbell]) 144
devilled eggs 122
dhal and egg curry 118
egg burta 124
egg curry 117
egg fritters 121
egg soup 69
fried whole eggs 119
kedgeree of fish 72
omelette Indian style 123
orange custard 140
poached eggs in milk 119
poached eggs with tomatoes 120
Princess Royal custard 139
puddings 142, 144, 146, 149, 152–3 155, 160, 163
rumbled eggs 121
sauces 45–50, 52–3

tomato soufflé 127
eggless date cake (Natalie) 171
endive or lettuce with cream 131

farines 22
fish 17, 71–81
baked sprats 78
baked and stuffed fish 80
bouillabaisse 80
excellent sauce for fish 50
fillets of fish à la Colbert 75
fish balls 79
fish curry 77
fried sprats 78
great-uncle Alick's fish pie 72
kedgeree of fish 72
oyster cocktail (for 4 glasses) 75
pickled fish 76
plain baked fish 78
prawn cutlets 73
ragout 76
sardine rolls 74
sardine savouries 79
smoked fish savoury 74
flash 222
flour, patent flour 166
food-poisoning, prevention 19
Francatelli, Charles Elmé, Francatelli's herb seasoning 28
French bean(s)
French beans à la Provençale 125
Mrs Shallard's way of bottling French beans 206
fritters, egg fritters 121
frosting 185
fruit
chicken curry with fruit 105
cold oven fruit cake 173
creamed ices for preserved fruit 144
crème supreme (Sophie Grisbach's recipe) 143
fruit creams 145
fruit pickles 211
good fruit cake (Natalie) 172
meat curry with fruit 88
see also specific fruit
fruit juice, water ices 142
fudge, caramel fudge (Mrs Harris) 189

gelatine 22
ghee 9, 26
gills 15
gin 223
ginger
ginger bread 1 (Mrs Currie) 181
ginger bread 2 (Mrs Gray) 182
ginger cake (Mrs Cahusac) 184
ginger rock 189
ginger snaps (rapa) 201
glacé icing 186
gnocchi 134
golden pudding 157
goose, stuffing for roast duck or goose 2 58
gooseberry
gooseberry chutney 207
gooseberry preserve 215
green gooseberry marmalade 206
Grant, James 12
gravy 59
fresh tomato gravy sauce for made dishes 54
gravy balls 58
gravy browning 35
Grisbach, Sophie, crème supreme 143

guava jelly and cheese 207
haddock, baked and stuffed fish 80
half-pay pudding 151
ham
  galantine of beef 84
  ham to boil 98
  tomatoes à la Provençale 1 126
Harvey's sauce 36
hash, China hash 96
herring
  mustard sauce for fresh herrings 51
  pickled fish 76
Highlands 11
Hindu's beef 85

ices
  creamed ices for preserved fruit 144
  ice cube coffee 220
  iced coffee 220
  iced sauce for asparagus 50
  water ices 142
  icing
  cream icing 186
  glacé icing 186
India 7, 8–9, 11, 12, 14
  weights and measures 15
Ingram, Mrs, Mrs Ingram's sponge 174

jam 205–17
  baked pudding 149
  black cap pudding 147
  cape gooseberry jam 215
  creamed ices for preserved fruit 144
  emergency chutney 209
  fruit creams 145
  sweet baked batter pudding 140
  Zandrina pudding 138
jelly
  banana jelly 154
  claret jelly 153
  guava jelly and cheese 207
  mint jelly 210
  orange jelly (Mrs Shallard) 213
  sago jelly 148
  tapioca jelly 148
Jimmy 95
Johnson, Mrs 207
julep, mint julep 222

Kashmir chutney 210
kedgeree of fish 72
ketchup
  mushroom ketchup 38
  walnut ketchup 37
kidney soup 66
Kidston, Mrs, tomato sauce 2 (Mrs Kidston) 34
kitcheree 111–12

lamb
  meat curry 87
  stuffings for 57
  see also mutton
lemon 206
  Aunt Louisa (pudding) 142
  baked pudding 149
  barley water 221
  essence of lemons 39
  glacé icing 186
  golden shred marmalade 214
  lemon barley water 222
  lemon cheesecake 160
  lemon pudding 160
  preserved lemon peel 217
  Swiss cakes 184
  tapioca jelly 148

lentil(s)
dhal churchurree 116
kitcheree 2 112
mess of pottage 63
mulligatawny soup 65
stewed dhal 114
see also dahl
lettuce 64, 81, 96
endive or lettuce with cream 131
pomelo salad with lettuce 128
lobster salad in aspic 81
Lorimer, Janet, chocolate cake 179

macaroons
macaroons (Mother's [Fanny Charlotte Campbell]) 202
walnut macaroons 203
mackerel, pickled fish 76
Madras 7
Madras curry powder 26
maître d'hôtel 53
Malay spice powder 30
malt biscuits 197
mango 101
mango chutney 210
marchpane (marzipan) 170
Margaret pudding 141
marmalade
golden pudding 157
golden shred marmalade 214
green gooseberry marmalade 206
Mrs Shallard's marmalade 213
marrow, fried marrow and tomato 128
mayonnaise
mayonnaise salad dressing without oil 45
mayonnaise sauce (Aberfoyle) 46
mayonnaise sauce 2 46
measures, Indian 15
meat 83–107
cooked meat curry 95
Jimmy 95
meat croquettes 94
meat curry 87
meat curry with fruit 88
meat moulds 22
meat roasted in a saucepan 91
pickle for meat 33
potted meat 86
meatballs, curried 90
meringue, coconut meringue for filling tartlets 150
mess of pottage 63
milk
milk puddings 22
milk punch (Mrs Sandeep) 221
salad dressings with condensed milk 49
mint
mint beer 222
mint chutney 211
mint jelly 210
mint julep 222
Morley, Mrs, sweet scones 168
mulligatawny soup 65
mundah 139
mushroom 126
mushroom ketchup 38
mustard 8
mustard sauce 2 51
mustard sauce for fresh herrings 51
mutton 87
China hash 96
meat curry 87
mutton baked with potatoes 99
mutton pilau 102

pish-pash 88
potato pie 113
stuffings for mutton 57
see also lamb

oatmeal 58
oatmeal and bacon stuffing 57
oatmeal scones 192
olla podrida 111
omelette Indian style 123
onion
onion sauce 52
spiced vinegar for pickled onions 32
orange
golden shred marmalade 214
Mrs Shallard's marmalade 213
orange cake 176–7
orange custard 140
orange jelly (Mrs Shallard) 213
orange salad for wild duck 135
orange syrup 55
preserved orange peel 217
ounces (ozs) 15
oyster cocktail (for 4 glasses) 75

Paris toast 119
parsley 8
essence of parsley 38–9
parsley sauce 54
pastry 22
baked pudding 149
banana puffs with mock cream 155
puff pastry 22
sardine rolls 74
short crust pastry for sweet tarts 22, 149, 200
suet pastry 22
pâté, imitation pâté de foie gras 86
patties, brain patties 89
peach
fruit creams 145
peach chutney 209
pearl barley 63
pea(s) 17, 132
China hash 96
peas à la Parisienne 125
peas preserved underground 213
stewed peas 124
pickles
fruit pickles 211
pickle for meat 33
pickled fish 76
spiced vinegar for pickled onions 32
pie(s)
bacon and egg pie 119
great-uncle Alick's fish pie 72
potato pie 113
rabbit pie 98
pikelets 201
pilau
mutton pilau 102
pilau (pellow) 100–1
'pinky pani' (potassium permanganate solution) 19
pish-pash 88
plum pudding, brandy sauce for 56
pomelo salad with lettuce 128
poor man's champagne 222
pork
meat curry 87
pork curry 97
potage bonne femme 64
potato 18
baked potato puff 129
beef or mutton baked with potatoes 99
beetroot as a full meal 128

chicken/duckling curry 104
great-uncle Alick's fish pie 72
meat roasted in a saucepan 91
mess of pottage 63
mixed vegetable soup 67
potato burta 110, 114
potato pie 113
potato scones 129, 193
potatoes maître d'hôtel 129
soup maigre 62
stuffing for roast duck or goose 2 58
vegetable curry 132
potted meat 86
poultry 83–107
prawn
prawn curry 8–9, 73
prawn cutlets 73
preserves 205–17
prune(s), stewed 158
puddings 137–63
Aunt Louisa (pudding) 142
baked pudding 149
black cap pudding 147
brandy sauce for plum pudding 56
chocolate pudding 146
Christmas pudding 162
coconut pudding 152
golden pudding 157
half-pay pudding 151
lemon pudding 160
Margaret pudding 141
stewing puddings 158
sweet baked batter pudding 140
toast and syrup pudding 159
treacle pudding 159
Xmas plum pudding (Mother's [Frances Charlotte Campbell]) 163
Zandrina pudding 138
puftaloons with bacon 133
pulled bread 196
pumpkin soup with croutons 68
punch, milk punch (Mrs Sandeep) 221

quince
quince conserve 1 216
quince conserve 2 (Enid Lorimer's) 216

rabbit pie 98
ragout 76
raisin(s) 100–1, 151–3, 162–3, 170, 185, 202, 207–10
baked raisin pudding 141
Raj 11
Rajasthan 7
ramekins, cheese ramekins 124
raspberry, fruit creams 145
relish, cucumber relish 212
rice
baked rice 147
chicken dumpode 98
kedgeree of fish 72
kitcheree 111–12
mixed vegetable soup 67
mutton pilau 102
pilau (pellow) 100–1
pish-pash 88
plain boiled rice 110
rice creams 161
rice and dhal 117
rock, ginger rock 189
rock cakes 182–3
rum
flash 222
milk punch (Mrs Sandeep) 221
rusks 198

sago jelly 148
salad dressings
American salad dressing 48
mayonnaise salad dressing without oil 45
salad dressings with condensed milk 49
salads
lobster salad in aspic 81
orange salad for wild duck 135
pomelo salad with lettuce 128
sauce for cucumber salad 47
sauce for salads 47
salmon trout
fish balls 79
plain baked fish 78
salt
cayenne salt 30
spice salt 27
sandwiches, tomato sandwiches 128
sardine
sardine rolls 74
sardine savouries 79
sauces 41–59
anchovy sauce 42
béchamel sauce 52
brandy sauce for plum pudding 56
bread sauce 52
cream béchamel 53
Cumberland sauce 44
excellent sauce for fish 50
fresh tomato gravy sauce for made dishes 54
Harvey's sauce 36
iced sauce for asparagus 50
maître d'hôtel 53
mayonnaise sauce (Aberfoyle) 46
mayonnaise sauce 2 46
mushroom ketchup 38
mustard sauce for fresh herrings 51
mustard sauce 2 51
onion sauce 52
parsley sauce 54
sauce for asparagus 49
sauce for cucumber salad 47
sauce piquante 43–4
sauce for salads 47
sauce for wild duck 53–4
sweet sauce 56
tartare sauce 46
tomato sauce for keeping 33
tomato sauce 2 (Mrs Kidston) 34
walnut ketchup 37
saug, vegetable saug 113
scones
breakfast scones 193
cheese scones (Mrs Child's recipe) 192
drop scones 200
oatmeal scones 192
potato scones 129, 193
sweet scones (Mrs Morley) 168
Scotland 12
seasoning, Francatelli's herb seasoning 28
seer (Indian measure) 15
Shallard, Mrs
date loaf 199
marmalade 213
orange jelly 213
walnut bread 199
way of bottling French beans 206
soufflés 18
brains soufflé 107
soufflé batter 21
tomato soufflé 127

soup 18, 61–9
egg soup 69
kidney soup 66
mess of pottage 63
mixed vegetable soup 67
mulligatawny soup 65
potage bonne femme 1 64
potage bonne femme 2 64
pumpkin soup with croutons 68
soup maigre 62
thickening 23
tomato pulp soup 66
spaghetti d'Espagne 130
spices 25–39
Malay spice powder 30
spice salt 27
spinach 64, 113
split pea(s), dhal and egg curry 118
sponge cake
arrowroot sponge (Mrs Palmer) 174
Mrs Ingram's sponge 174
sponge cake 169
three minute sponge 175
sprat(s)
baked sprats 78
fried sprats 78
pickled fish 76
steak, baked steak 91
stewing puddings 158
stocks 23
strawberry, fruit creams 145
stuffings 41–59
oatmeal and bacon stuffing 57
stuffed tripe 106
stuffing for roast duck 1 57
stuffing for roast duck or goose 2 58
suet 58, 80, 85, 98, 141, 151, 153, 157, 159, 162–3
sultana(s) 88, 100–1, 105, 151, 162–3, 169–70, 173, 182, 185, 207–9
Sutton, Mrs, Mrs Sutton's tea cake 167
sweet sauce 56
Swiss cakes 184
Swiss roll 183
syrup, orange syrup 55

table of proportions 21–3
tablespoons 15
tapioca jelly 148
tartare sauce 46
tartlets, coconut meringue for filling tartlets 150
tea cakes
Aunt Charley's tea cake 167
Mrs Sutton's tea cake 167
thickening 23
tired housewife's cake 169
toast
cheese toast 135
Paris toast 119
toast and syrup pudding 159
toffee
cream toffee 187
Russian toffee (Mrs Cahusac) 187
tomato
fresh tomato chutney 212
fresh tomato gravy sauce for made dishes 54
fried marrow and tomato 128
poached eggs with tomatoes 120
spaghetti d'Espagne 130
stuffed tomatoes 126
tomato custards 127
tomato pulp soup 66
tomato sandwiches 128
tomato sauce for keeping 33

tomato sauce 2 (Mrs Kidston) 34
tomato sauce 3 35
tomato soufflé 127
tomatoes à la Provençale 126–7
tomatoes and parsley 125
treacle pudding 159
tripe, stuffed tripe 106
trout
plain baked fish 78
see also salmon trout
Tully, Sir Mark 11
turnip 62–3, 96
blanquette of turnips 131

Umbeyla campaign 12
Uncle Tom 153

vanilla cream 155
vegetables 17
mixed vegetable soup 67
vegetable curry 132
vegetable saug 113
vegetable and savoury dishes 109–35
see also specific vegetables
vermicelli 69
vinegar 31
spiced vinegar for pickled onions 32
vinegar cake 185

walnut 171
walnut bread (Mrs Shallard) 199
walnut ketchup 37
walnut macaroons 203
water biscuits 195
water ices 142
weights and measures 15
whisky 223
white cake 185
white sauce, cucumber with white sauce 131
wholemeal cake (Mrs Maclaren) 178
wine substitute 223

Xmas plum pudding (Mother's [Frances Charlotte Campbell]) 163

Zandrina pudding 138

About the Author

Coming from Sussex where **Bryony Hill** was also educated, after a year at Brighton College of Art, she spent four years in France after which, on returning to England, she met and eventually married the television sports presenter Jimmy Hill. Her tenth book – *An Indian Table* – is inspired by *Scotland to Shalimar – a Family's Life in India,* which followed the lives of her mother's family six generations of whom were born in India. Apart from writing Bryony is a keen gardener, painter and cook and, when she came across a collection of her great-great grandmother's and great-grandmother's recipes, the seed was sown to dig deep into her ancestors' history and lives.

Acknowledgements

2020 was a year to forget but, because I had ample time on my hands I was fortunate enough to put together *An Indian Table – a Family's Recipes during the Raj*, a companion book to *Scotland to Shalimar – a Family's Life in India.* I couldn't have done it without the help, advice, encouragement and enthusiasm once again from Heather Boisseau, Clare Christian and Anna Burtt, the team at RedDoor Press. Thank you for making this such an enjoyable and rewarding project during difficult times for us all.

Find out more about RedDoor Press and sign up to our newsletter to hear about our **latest releases, author events,** exciting **competitions** and more at

reddoorpress.co.uk

YOU CAN ALSO FOLLOW US:

@RedDoorBooks

Facebook.com/RedDoorPress

@RedDoorBooks